On High

YORKSHIRE HILLS

Exploring the "Two Thousand Footers"

by Phil Clayton

First Published in Great Britain 1993 by
Dalesman Publishing Company Limited,
Stable Courtyard, Broughton Hall,
Skipton, North Yorkshire BD23 3AE

ISBN 1 85568 059 9
Typeset by **Lands Services, East Molesey, Surrey.**
Printed and bound by **Redwood Books Ltd.**

Contents

Dedication

To the memory of Margaret Spinks.

Acknowledgements

I would like to thank my wife for her good sense in coming from Yorkshire and my in-laws for providing a Yorkshire home from home which was the base for so much of the walking described here.

Thanks are also due to Maria Nicholson for the drawings of Great Shunner Fell and the Howgills.

Several friends have walked these high hills with me and I thank them for their companionship.

1
Yorkshire's Two-Thousanders

A glance at an atlas will show that Yorkshire's lowland broad acres are balanced out by as many high ones of hill, moor and mountain. The county's lowland reaches, tracking the main river valleys, are encompassed to north, and particularly west, by high land while even the vales have their upthrusts. In the fairest parts of the county it is the juxtaposition of dale and fellside which gives the essential contrast to the scene. This work describes the 2,000-foot summits of Yorkshire in the hope that it encourages others to seek out the county's highlights. It should be noted that the author does not recognise the metrication of mountains so that altitudes are given in feet and distances in miles.

The hills explored in this work are all to be found in the real Yorkshire, that is the Yorkshire of superlatives which existed in geography lessons when I was at school and which was chopped about by bureaucratic decree on April 1, 1974 – a significant choice of date. Indeed, were the present-day boundaries to be used, the scope of this book would be somewhat lessened as Yorkshire has 'lost' eleven of its two-thousanders, eight to Cumbria and three to County Durham, including its highest summit! Boundaries tend to follow natural features and so it is not surprising that seven of the tops lie on the present county boundary and are therefore shared with other counties so that it is possible, on High Seat for instance, to leap backwards and forwards between Yorkshire and Cumbria. It is as well to check that not too many people are watching this exhibition, though the sheep don't seem to mind. Before 1974, eight summits were shared with other counties. If this sounds too complicated then table two at the end of the book might help! It's only people who make things complex. The fells themselves stay as open and straightforward as ever, wherever the bureaucrats may decide to put them.

There is no agreement as to how many two-thousanders there actually are in Yorkshire, for different authorities have used different methods of defining them. For some the mere presence of a contour ring has been deemed sufficient whilst others have developed rather complex mathematical formulae offsetting height-difference against distance. The Ordnance Survey has complicated the issue by going metric and by resurveying the countryside, subtly altering the altitudes of some fells. So, what follows is a personal list of three dozen tops. Some may disagree with it and that is their prerogative; however, I would encourage them to go and check on the ground and not just on the map!

The 36 two-thousanders in the county range in height from 2,585 feet down to 2,000, the latter being the shrinking Birks Fell! Some are high and mighty, fells which stir the blood by their grandeur and which richly deserve the title mountain. Some are little more than grassy or peaty mounds on a broad ridge and only their height separates them from the hills. On some of the summits on certain days of the year you may scarcely be able to move for folk, on others on

Yorkshire's High Fells :- locations of summits.

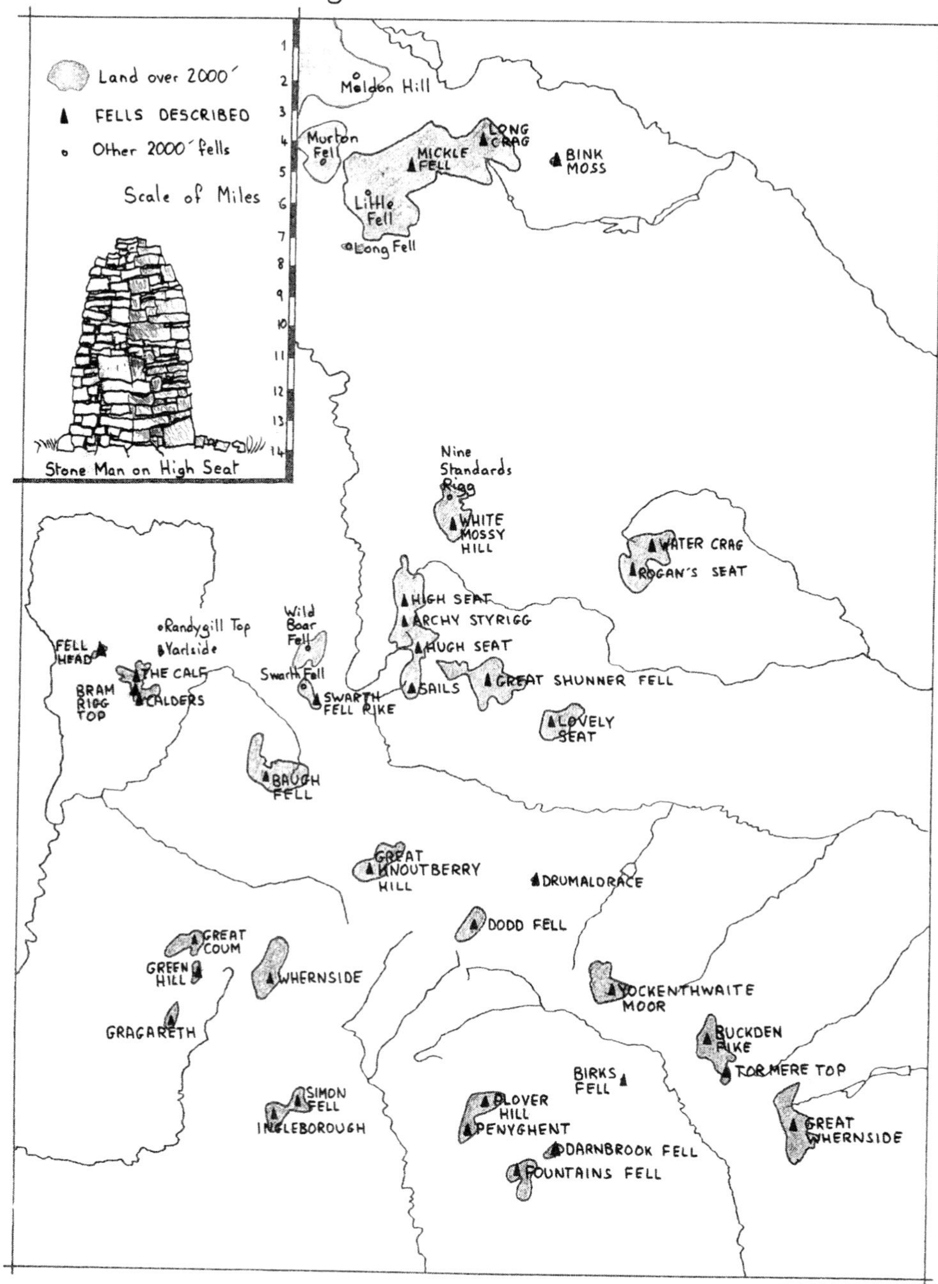

any day of the year you will be unlikely to meet anyone. Some tops are marked by triangulation pillars, cairns, shelters and, regrettably, rubbish, while others are unmarked and may well take some finding. Some have paths of almost motorway proportions to their summits, others stand pathless in the midst of heather or peat. Some stand close together and several tops can be visited on

Shepherd's cairn – Archy Styrigg, on the borders of Yorkshire and Cumbria.

Summit cairn – Fountains Fell, looking towards Great Whernside.

one walk, one or two stand proudly isolated. There is much of variety among the high Yorkshire fells and they are all certainly worth visiting.

This is not primarily written as a guidebook though I have described routes which I have enjoyed following, and anyway the best guide of all is produced by the Ordnance Survey. A map is a constant delight for the visitor to the hills, an

Yorkshire's High Fells :- physical features.

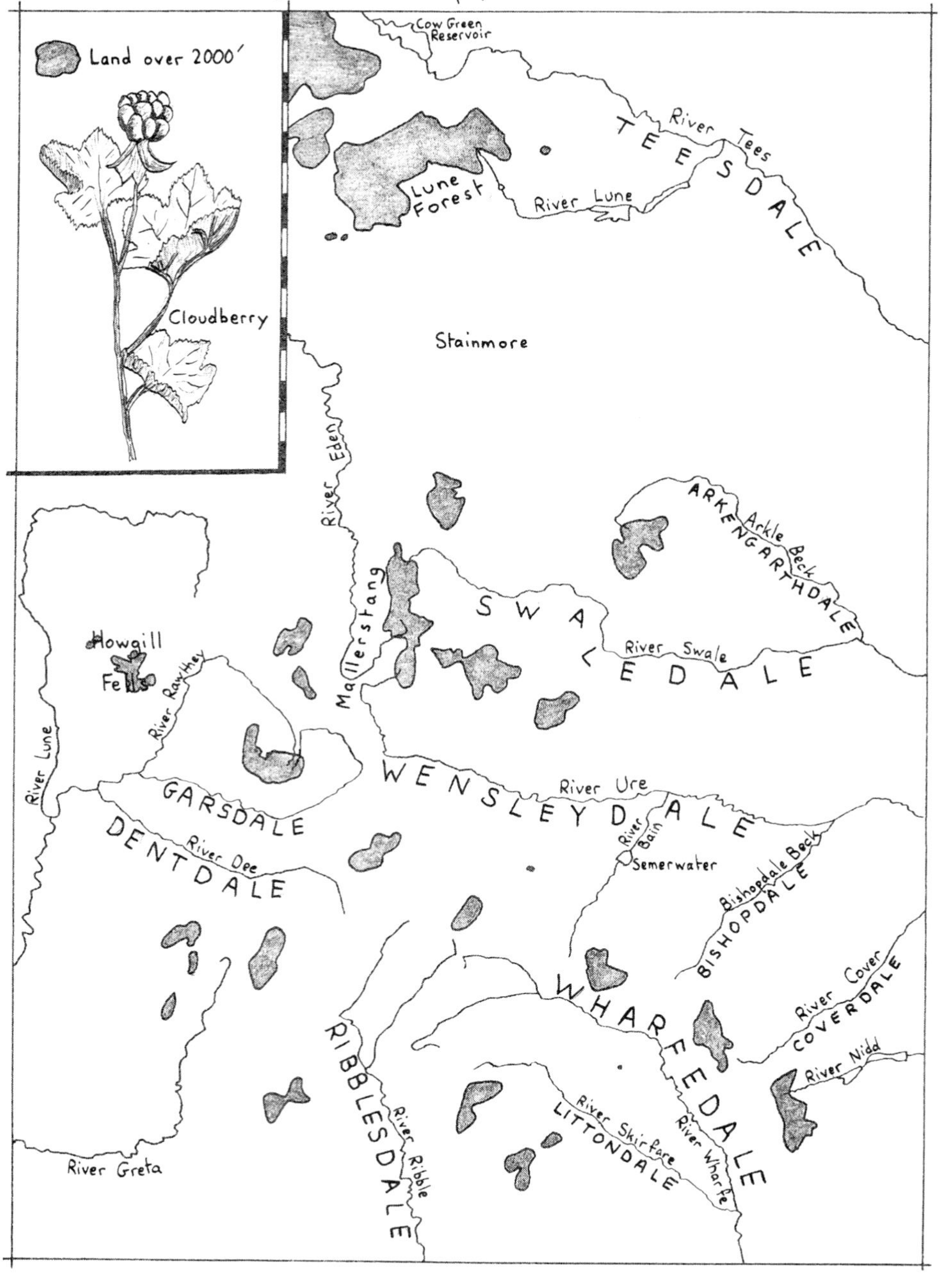

Yorkshire's High Fells :- communications.

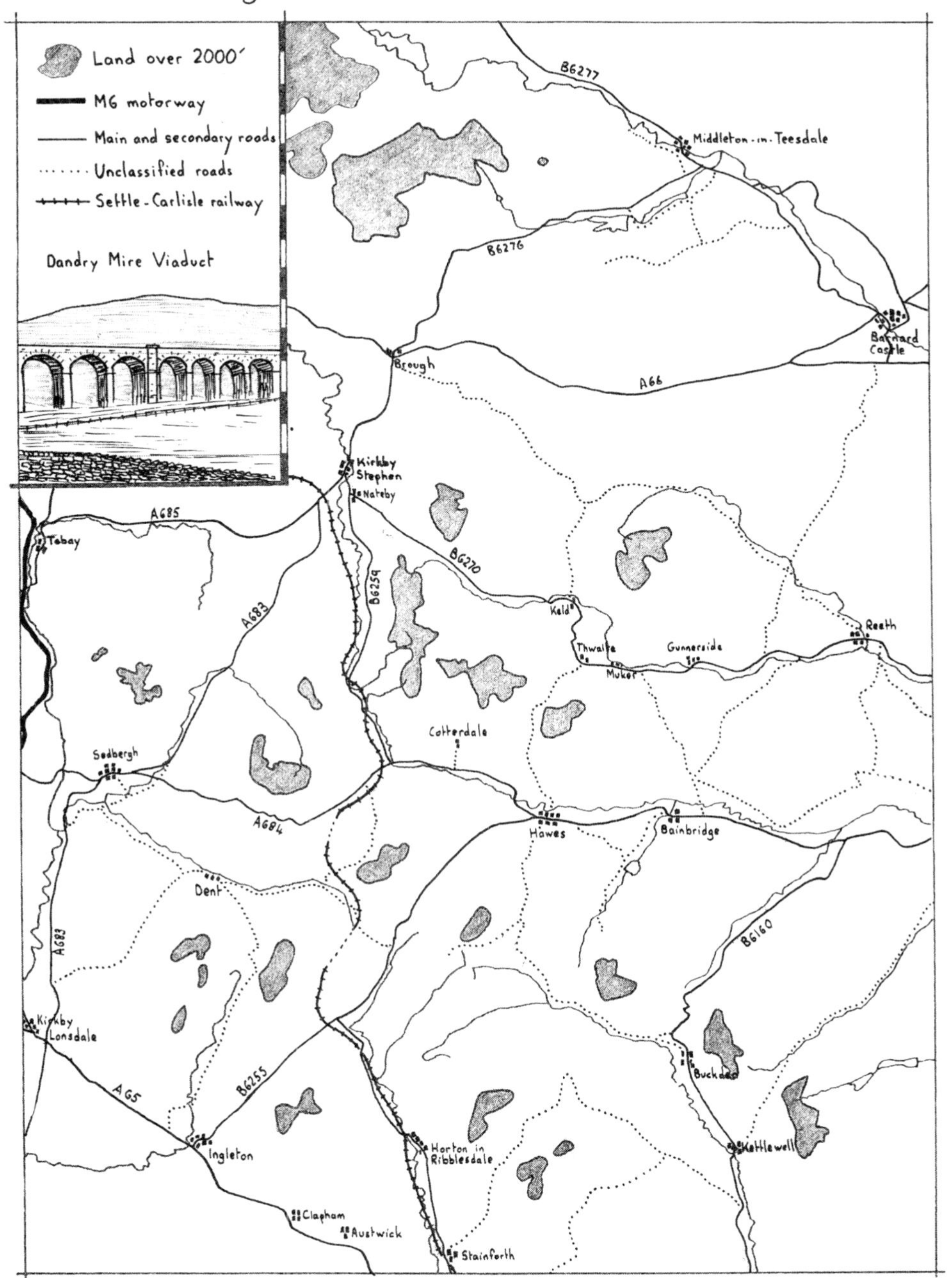

inspiration before, a reassurance during, and a souvenir after a walk. Many of the more popular upland areas of Yorkshire are now covered by the O.S. Outdoor Leisure series of sheets which, at a scale of 1:25000, or about 2½ inches to the mile, provides a wealth of detail even down to such features as walls and fences. On the top of Great Knoutberry Hill in driving rain and twenty

Ingleborough – the best-known of Yorkshire's "high hills". A classic view from the scars above Thornton-in-Lonsdale. (Geoffrey N. Wright)

yards visibility, this can be a great comfort! The Landranger series, at half the detail of the Outdoor Leisure maps, are also excellent walker's maps and give a clear idea of the wider landscape. Both of these maps show public rights-of-way where the walker has a legal right of passage even though, in some cases, there may be no path visible in front of the feet. As an aid to the location of the hills, a list of grid references and Ordnance Survey maps is given in table one.

A few of the summits mentioned in this book can be reached by public right-of-way but most of them lie off legal routes. It behoves the walker to respect the fact that private land is being traversed and no matter how poor or neglected the terrain appears, it is of economic significance to the landowner or farmer. Most of the area described in this work is sheep farming country and the walker may be fortunate enough to meet a farmer or shepherd as he goes about his work either on foot or, more likely these days, on a motor cycle or all-terrain vehicle. These three- and four-wheeled crosses between a trail bike and a miniature tractor have been a great boon to the hill farmer and are certainly kinder to the fellsides than the bikes which they are replacing. No one will ever build a machine to replace the sheepdog and it is a delight to sit and watch these skilful and intelligent animals at work.

Some of the fells are important grouse moors which will be under the gun from the twelfth of August. Two are under the gun for much longer as they fall within the bounds of the Warcop artillery ranges.

The three dozen fells described here, while all belonging to the Yorkshire Pennines, can be grouped together because of geography, geology or history into smaller and, for the visitor, more manageable groups. A sketch-map is included for each section, to put into context the places and features mentioned therein. This is not meant as a substitute for the maps of the Ordnance Survey: the sketch-map sketches the outlines, the OS fills in the details.

The most remote bunch of tops lies around Yorkshire's wildest boundary, a 25-mile border of moor and moss which meanders across some of the least known land in England. Only three roads cross this boundary line and there are but two habitations within half a mile of it, the remote farm of Birkdale lying near the River Tees and the Tan Hill Inn. This, the highest in England, was transferred together with much of the ground described below into County Durham in 1974. The Boundary Commission recommended the inn's return to Yorkshire in 1989. Let us hope that this is the beginning of a restitution of all the lost areas of Yorkshire's far north-west.

Trig points and mapping

The trig points or triangulation pillars referred to in this book are just some of about six thousand such columns, many of which are to be found on, or near to, the summit of hills. They were built for triangulation purposes from 1935 when the Ordnance Survey established a new triangulation of Great Britain. The pillars are constructed of concrete or local stone and each required a couple of tons of material to be carried to the site!

This most welcome mountain top monolith conceals as much as it reveals (see diagram). Many trig points and their surroundings are painted white to assist in aerial surveys. The Centre Mark is the heart of the column, being a brass bolt embedded in concrete, and all measurements refer to it. The centre pipe is revealed by removing a plug in the centre of the "spider", the three grooves which hold the surveyor's theodolite on top of the pillar. The pipe is used to centralise the theodolite by being the recipient of a plumb line which can be seen to be central over the mark by looking through the sighting tubes. Three of these are usually cemented over but one is left open for drainage. The lower centre mark locates the exact position of the Trig Point so that it can be rebuilt in case of damage.

The mapping of the land is of particular interest to all walkers who rely upon the accuracy of the cartographers from the Ordnance Survey. As its name suggests, the O.S. was started as a branch of the army in the eighteenth century when it was realised that few really accurate maps of Britain existed. Earlier attempts at mapping had resulted in pictorially pleasing (hence the number of framed reproductions found in pubs!) but not especially useful sheets. These attempted to locate settlements, rivers and so on but took little notice of upland areas, treating them with the same kind of "here be monsters" vagueness that early world cartographers used about the further reaches of the oceans.

Present Ordnance Survey maps of mountain and moorland areas are based on the 1:10560 (now converted to 1:10000) scale survey. This works out at an imperial scale of six inches to one mile (now metricated to ten centimetres to one kilometre). Maps of urban areas, minor towns and cultivated areas are derived from larger scale surveys. The "Six Inch" maps were originally drawn up during the nineteenth century. Since 1969 the new, metric, revised sheets have been published at 1:10000 and in some areas have replaced "Six Inch" maps which had not been revised since before 1939!

The old "Six Inch" maps were of vital importance in respect of what mountaineers hold so dear – they were the basis for contours which are not shown on larger scale maps. Contouring was first used on the original six inch survey of Ireland (1839-40) and was adopted for Great Britain after 1853.

Contours however have been more subject to changes of policy than most other O.S. map features, both in respect of method and of the Vertical Interval at which they were instrumentally surveyed. For instance, while lower lying places were contoured at V.I.'s of twenty-five or fifty feet, land above 1,000 feet was often levelled at intervals of 250 or 500 feet, or not at all instrumentally.

There was also little uniformity between different parts of the country, so that while Wales and most of England (south of Lancashire and Yorkshire) were surveyed instrumentally up to 1,000 feet, Lancashire was levelled up to 2,600 feet at 200 foot intervals and sketched contours were drawn in at 25 feet intervals up to 2,625. (The Old Man of Coniston is just 10 feet higher.) In Yorkshire, land over 1,200 feet was surveyed at 400 foot intervals up to 2,400: Whernside being 2416 feet on the original survey.

Above 1,000 feet then some areas were levelled accurately but Wales and southern England were contoured by a quicker, cheaper but less accurate method known as water levelling. The basic contouring programme for England and Wales – some parts of Scotland remained contourless for much longer – was completed in 1891. Other changes added to the mish-mash. Extra contours were drawn in at interpolated (guessed?) intervals, while between 1909 and 1912 the contours were printed blue!

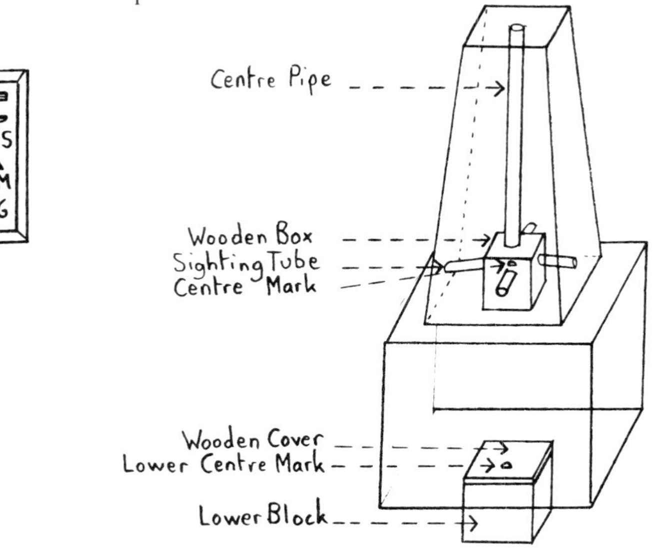

The Davidson Committee, which reported in 1938 on many aspects of Ordnance Survey policy and practice, stated that "... the accuracy of the work conforms to certain well defined limits ... a minute precision ... is not required ..." This led to the recommendation that contours on the "six inch" map should be surveyed at twenty-five foot intervals and that the same data should be included on 1:25000 scale maps. On the last "six inch" sheets there is a mixture of information from different sources. As might be expected, nineteenth century contours were found to be most accurate in areas of low relief so that in mountainous and hilly areas the main source of contours has latterly been the air survey – the development of this technique has greatly accelerated the work of re-contouring.

The 1:10000 scale series which is designed to replace the "six inch" maps commenced publication in 1969. The survey for the basic maps at the new scale began in the Scottish Highlands, while in other parts of the country the maps are being produced by conversion from the "six inch" Regular Series. Height values are given in metres (2,000 feet corresponds to 609.60741 metres!) and contour datum is again derived from the usual mixed bag of sources. As information from the new survey has found its way onto 1:25000 and 1:50000 maps, one or two changes and anomolies have been thrown up. One top, poor old Birks Fell, has been struck off! It's not even 2000 feet any more! Still, in the geological scale mountains are only fairly temporary phenomena anyway and, as Isaiah said ..."every mountain and hill should be made low".

2
North-West Frontier

As a river name, Lune is probably more familiar on t'other side o' t'ills in Lancashire than it is in Yorkshire, and this is not surprising as the eastward-flowing Lune runs for only a little over ten miles from source to its confluence with the Tees between Middleton and Mickleton. Grassholme and Selset reservoirs give graphic evidence of the water-gathering ability of the valley whose upper reaches, a desolation of peat hag and mire, is known as Lune Forest. This was no doubt named a forest in the old hunting sense rather than as a thickly wooded area although the remains of trees have been found in the peat hereabouts up to quite a high level. Nowadays anyway it scarcely carries a tree. The northern edge of the Lune Forest, and the river's northern watershed, has three of Yorkshire's 2,000-foot hills along its broad ridge and it seems right to start with Mickle Fell, Yorkshire's highest summit.

Mickle Fell

Mickle Fell, 2,585 feet, the name means, appropriately enough, the big fell, must be one of the most 'in' mountains in England. It's in the Warcop artillery range boundary, in the Upper Teesdale National Nature Reserve and in a grouse shooting area, all of which means it is 'out' as far as the humble pedestrian is concerned.

The Warcop ranges cover 25,000 acres centred on Little Fell, a couple of miles to the west. Although the "impact area" is quite small, limited to Roman Fell and Long Fell, the "danger area" is big enough to cover even the most careless of shots and walkers who stray out of Yorkshire to venture further west than Mickle Fell will become accustomed to seeing quantities of what look like large vacuum flasks lying around in various stages of twisted destruction or rusting decomposition. The military authority is scrupulous in marking the bounds of its range with large red signs displaying the comforting warning not to touch anything "as it may explode and kill you". A red flag flies at entry points to the range whenever firing is taking place and the crump of shells can be heard for miles. The "danger area" limits are clearly marked on the appropriate Ordnance Survey sheets. Monday is generally an off day and it is a wonderful experience to savour the peace which is to be found when it is the closed season on a firing range.

I once walked to Mickle Fell from the Westmorland side, crossing a large chunk of the artillery range. It is a wild country once the heights have been gained and a wide one in contrast to the rather hemmed-in valley of Swindale Beck which is followed on the ascent from Hilton. On my route, which meandered out of the county to find various interesting but non-Yorkshire summits, Little Fell had to be crossed before Mickle Fell could be gained and the two face each other, Little Fell belying its name which must surely have been given it as a joke, across the waste of the Lune Forest. Here is some of the roughest land in England, the slopes falling down to the Lune across a corrugation of peat hags and groughs. Usually the greenery on top of the hags is more prominent than the dark brown of the groughs but here dun predominates.

Maize Beck, Upper Teesdale, with Mickle Fell – Yorkshire's highest mountain – beyond.
(Geoffrey N. Wright)

The Upper Teesdale fells from near Birkdale, looking towards Cross fell (on right, in distance).
(Geoffrey N. Wright)

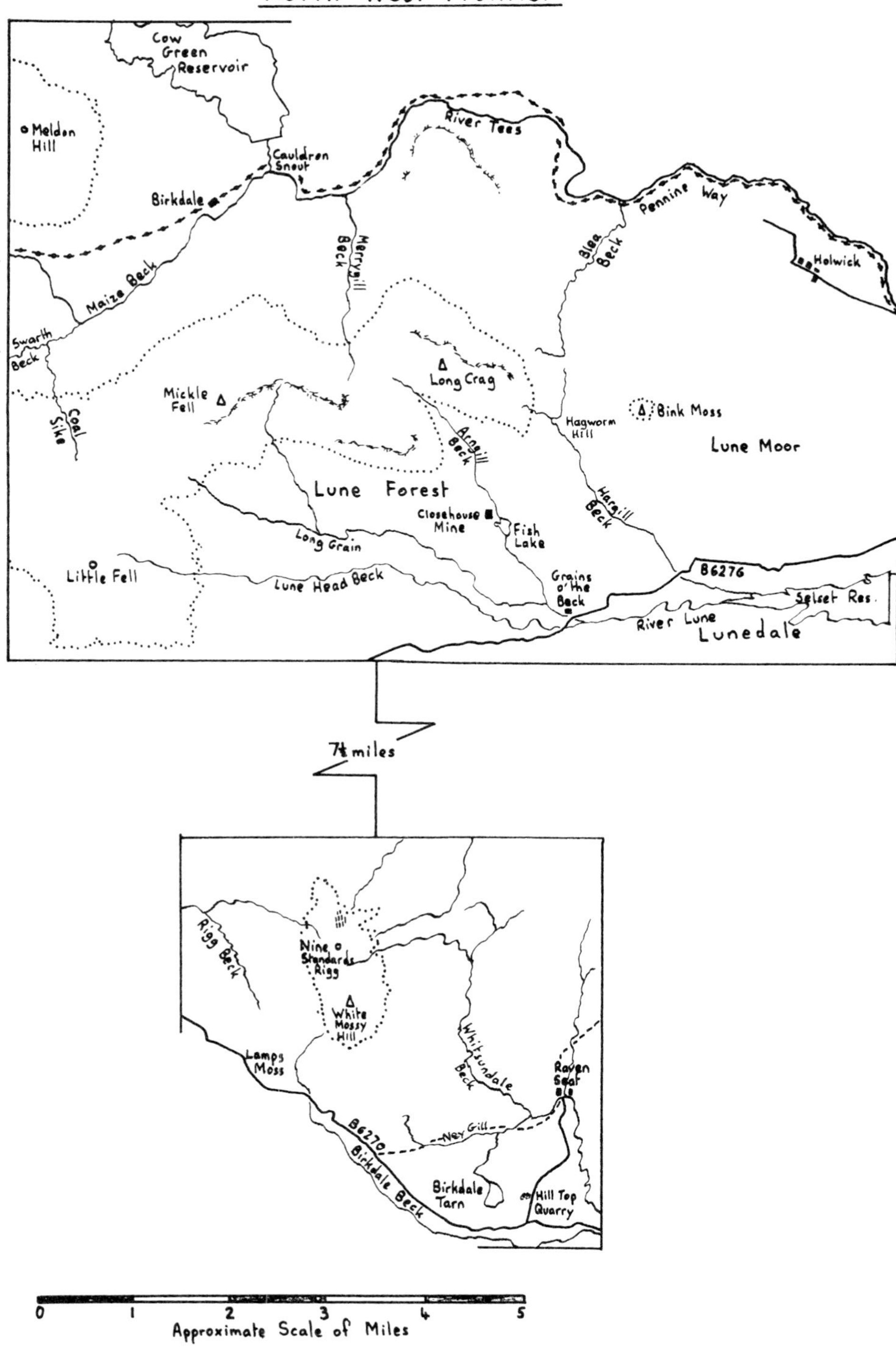
North West Frontier
Cow Green Reservoir
Meldon Hill
Cauldron Snout
River Tees
Birkdale
Pennine Way
Holwick
Merrygill Beck
Blea Beck
Maize Beck
Swarth Beck
Long Crag
Mickle Fell
Bink Moss
Hagworm Hill
Coal Sike
Arngill Beck
Lune Moor
Lune Forest
Hargill Beck
Closehouse Mine
Fish Lake
Long Grain
B6276
Little Fell
Lune Head Beck
Grains o' the Beck
Selset Res.
River Lune
Lunedale
7¼ miles
Rigg Beck
Nine Standards Rigg
White Mossy Hill
Whitsundale Beck
Lamps Moss
Raven Seat
B6270
Ney Gill
Birkdale Beck
Birkdale Tarn
Hill Top Quarry
0 1 2 3 4 5
Approximate Scale of Miles
2000 foot contour

The forest is drained by a multiplicity of streams having the appearance, on the map at least, of the spreading branches of a wind-bent tree. Goal Sike, Force Beck, Long Grain and Connypot Beck meet to form the Lune proper hard on Grains o' th' Beck Bridge where an inn once welcomed travellers on the lonely road between Brough and Middleton. Down there in the valley is Fish Lake, a forgotten tarn by a barytes mine. The worst of the mire can be avoided by keeping to the broad, curving ridge top which links the two fells and encircles the head of the Lune Forest.

To the north, Coal Sike and Fisher Sike flow down to join Maize Beck, another tributary of the Tees. In the days before I had much sense I once cut across the headwaters of Coal Sike on a direct line from Mickle Fell to Murton Fell. It is not an exercise which I intend repeating for I have seldom crossed such a strength-sapping, boot-drenching, morale-lowering stretch of land. The grouse, with their staccato call of "go back, go back", have never given such sound advice.

Maize Beck follows a course punctuated by a series of virtually right-angled bends, suggesting that the drainage pattern in this area has been disrupted. A study of the map certainly seems to point to a former westward flow for what are now the beck's headwaters rising between Backstone Edge and Meldon Hill. It is rather a pity that these waters have been diverted for if they flowed over High Cup Nick they would certainly make a pretty waterfall.

For the last two miles of its course, to its confluence with the Tees, Maize beck marks the boundary between Yorkshire and Westmorland while the Tees itself divides Yorkshire from County Durham for the rest of its journey to the North Sea. They say that a sportsman once shot a brace of grouse at this junction of the three counties. He was standing in County Durham and his left-hand bird fell into Yorkshire while the right-hand grouse dropped into Westmorland. Alas, since 1974, such a feat could no longer be repeated.

A number of stone men stands along the Little Fell – Mickle Fell ridge: shepherds' cairns which often appear more prominent from below than from close by, and the remains of a stone structure which gives shelter to the sheep whose heaf these wind-blown peaty acres are.

Although the walker has plenty of time on the approach to study the final climb up on to Mickle Fell's summit, it is still sudden and steep and takes the walker from the peat ridge to the bare fell top where the heather is replaced by close-cropped grasses. Lying as it does in an area long famed for its plant life and now firmly established within the Upper Teesdale National Nature Reserve, the top of Mickle Fell has attracted the attention of botanists and is the home of some rare survivals from the times of the ice ages. Although it was formerly believed that the tops of the highest fells protruded through the ice sheet as 'nunataks', thus preserving their flora, this theory has been superseded and the Teesdale rarities are now thought to be the remains of species which previously covered a far greater extent at the end of the last glaciation and have retreated to survive as relicts. The Mickle Fell summit plateau is home to the general run of bilberry, cowberry, sheep's fescue, mountain fescue, brown bent and wavy hair grass as well as the less common 'reindeer moss' lichens, Iceland Moss lichen and Stiff Sedge.

On the southern side, around the head of the Lune Forest, where bands of limestone have given rise to crags and scree and sweeter soils, further interesting plants are to be found including alpine forget-me-not, the beautiful blue spring gentian, the white spring sandwort and Dovedale moss while the delicate starry saxifrage grows in damp flushes on the higher parts of the fell.

A wire fence is crossed as the escarpment becomes less steep and at last we are in Yorkshire. I was once going to follow the fence down to the valley when I noticed a line of specks along it. Closer inspection through my monocular revealed a line of beaters who were slowly working their way up the Maize Beck valley. They were driving the grouse towards the guns stationed in the groughs around the confluence of Coal Sike and Swarth Beck and a little later I heard the reports.

Some time after, descending to the head of Hilton Beck, I came across a black and white spaniel which was alternately growling and whimpering. The poor, brave soul had been left behind to guard the gun cases and walking sticks and looked as if it had been there for a long time carrying out its lonely vigil. Further down the valley I came across the shooting party's transport parked on a knoll overlooking the old lead mines, a fine collection of four-wheel drive vehicles including the Landrover of the Warcop Artillery Range Officer. A man who obviously likes shooting – even on a Monday when the bigger pieces are silent.

The top of Mickle Fell is larger than the foreshortened view gained from the ridge would suggest and quite flat. A walk of a quarter of a mile or so across this featureless plateau brings the visitor to the cairn, Yorkshire's crowning glory: the county summit. It is a substantial cairn with a shelter big enough for several tykes to seek refuge in and on one visit there was an empty beer bottle protruding from it. John Smith's of course.

The view repays careful study for it is both good on close-range detail and far-reaching in its wider scope although, as on any plateau top, the view from the edge is finer. Near at hand are Cow Green Reservoir and the hamlet of Harwood with its scatter of white-painted farms and barns. After a few days of rain the sight of the water surging over the dam and cascading down Cauldron Snout is a dramatic one with the white water standing out against the greens and duns of the surroundings. Further to the north, beyond the high road which joins Teesdale and Alston, is the Burnhope Seat ridge, another fine area of wild walking, but in County Durham. Eastwards is the long curve of Mickle Fell itself with its limestone crags hanging over the boggy waste draining down to Selset reservoir. This is not visible from the summit but the more distant one at Balderhead is. Of particular delight is the view south, along the deep valley of Mallerstang which frames the Three Peaks at its far end, and these sharply scarped mountains are in contrast to the dumpy Howgills further to the west. Little Fell looms large to the south-west and the Lake District fells fill the far western horizon. Finally in this 360° turn come the wastes of Murton Fell and the broad upper valley of Maize Beck with the high Pennines behind.

The only real blot, and this is adopting a most forgiving attitude towards Cow Green, is the radar station on Great Dun Fell. Still, you can always turn round quickly at that point. An interesting way of whiling away a bit of time on Mickle Fell's summit, whilst eating the butties and admiring the view, is to work out how many of those fells are in Yorkshire. The conscientious walker, blessed with a clear day and a good map, should be able to reel off at least a score.

A walk of just over a mile along the top of the escarpment leads the visitor to the trig point which bears the Ordnance Survey benchmark S10794. On the way between the two summits, broken bits of aluminium indicating the remains of a crashed aircraft, one of several to have come down on the Yorkshire Pennines, and a hut which was obviously a fairly substantial affair are passed. The limestone reaches a higher altitude on Mickle Fell than anywhere else in the county and several large shake holes have formed in the vicinity of the trig point.

Christmas on the High Fells

THE highest point in Yorkshire (Mickle Fell, 2591 ft., by the springs of the river Tees) is often particularly stormy. "Nine months o' winter and three months o' cold weather" is a bitter but justified taunt. From October to June, the mountain is apt to be ice-shackled, snow-piled and gale-swept. In this amazing Pennine country, the lowest meadow in a vast parish may be a thousand feet above sea-level, and so gripped by frost that even the hardiest cattle or sheep fail to survive outdoors.

Considerably higher are the scattered sheep-farms, sportsmen's inns, shepherds' and game-keepers' cottages — as well as the active mine-works with their caretaker or full-time gangs. These people are probably the most isolated of England's winter garrisons. One jocular ganger claimed that "these are the sort of places where everybody should take a spade to bed in winter. A shift of blast might blow in two yards o' snow-dust between bed and door."

I was a youth when I made the first Christmas crossing of Mickle Fell from the (then) Grains i' th' Beck inn on the Brough road by way of Maize Beck, Birkdale Farm, High Cup Nick to Hilton and Appleby.

Though dawn came slow, the weather was calm and clear. I had already made the crossing in summer so that the landmarks were familiar, not strange. Clear of the inn farm I soon became accustomed to the frosty air. Out on the open shoulder, the snow is firm and progress easy.

After a dull hour the day brightens up, and I halt to fix the necessary sun-glasses. The rising altitude of 2,000, 2,250 and 2,500 ft. also adds to the exhilaration. The angle of the ascent steepens, and in a while the snow-covered top is within reach. Hitherto I have faced the slope: now the leagues of white moor fall away, wrinkled here and there where heather and bent grass have shaped a cove; with level marshes hidden by the snow mask.

In my summer crossing of this long stretch of moorland I had felt crushed and rather lonely, though there was the calling of grouse, golden plover and other wild birds; sounds of sheep and cattle, and the soft prattle of descending brooks. Today all was white silence with birds and animals withdrawn, and bogs and marshes frozen stiff.

If before I had felt like an intruder, the feeling now approached alarm. Crossfell, Dufton Fell, and many another white summit fringed the immense shelf. I was sufficiently hardy to realise that it was a matter of nerves; that after every half-hour the Maize Beck and the twin Birkdale farms seemed and were nearer.

W.T. Palmer
(The Dalesman, December 1952)

As mentioned before, the summit of Yorkshire's highest fell cannot be gained by rights-of-way and the fact that it is in a firing range and a nature reserve make access a little difficult. This probably accounts for the fact that patriotic Yorkshire folk have hardly blazed a trail to the top and there is still an element of pioneering present on any excursion to the fell. This is probably preferable to what has happened to that surrogate county top, Ingleborough. There are, however, several public footpaths to lead the walker to the general vicinity of Mickle Fell whence a choice of route may lead upwards.

The most frequented is the track followed by the Pennine Way from the Tees. This runs up the Maize Beck valley past the remote farm at Birkdale and the ruins of Moss Shop but unfortunately it is on the north side of the beck which can carry a lot of water. A bridleway runs on the Yorkshire side of the Tees between Holwick and the Maize Beck just south of Birkdale. There it disappears from the map only to reappear a mile further upstream at the bottom of the county boundary fence. In the middle of the non-right-of-way stretch are the scant remains of Maizebeck Shop. When the lead mines were being worked it was too far for the miners to return daily to their homes further down the valley and so they would stay at the mine. There are several other 'shops' in the area indicating the miner's lodgings, the nearest being across the beck at Moss Shop. The bridleway just mentioned can be followed from Hilton on the Westmorland side as far as the boundary fence. This route will appeal to industrial archaeologists, particularly in its early stages along the deeply cut Scordale Beck and there is always the danger that those with a mining bent may never get past Amber Hill!

Another right-of-way, and one which is easier to follow on the map than on the ground, runs between Forest-in-Teesdale and the B6276 Brough to Middleton road. The path is intermittently visible if followed from the south where it runs alongside Hargill Beck to Hagworm Hill. Here it has to be deserted and the next of Yorkshire's north-west frontier trio of tops, Long Crag, can be crossed on the way to Mickle Fell. At least this approach has the virtue of being the in the real county from start to finish and, as on most routes to the county high spot, the lone walker can be fairly certain of being just that.

Long Crag

Long Crag, 2,250 feet, is not one of Yorkshire's better-known fells and its summit, unlike that of Mickle Fell two miles away to the west, is marked by only a small cairn.

The fell was most likely named from the Tees Valley for the crag, such as it is, is more visible from the north. Long Crag is really an eastern extension of Mickle Fell and, should the walk be continued to the county summit, a low wall of boulders, called The Old Dike, will be passed near the source of Arngill Beck. The two fells are joined at the wet and black morasses around Arngill Head Brocks. An interesting and descriptive name which means the brooks or headwaters of the eagle's stream. At one time this might have been the home of such magnificent birds but now it is the territory of quite another.

This is grouse shooting country *par excellence* and the walker is never far from reminders of the sport. There is a line of butts beside the path from the B6276 road, where it dips down to ford Hargill Beck and another one along the top of Staple Moss, Long Crag's broad and wet southern ridge. Avian evidence beside the path late one October indicated that more grouse had been shot than retrieved. I once met the Earl of Strathmore's gamekeeper on neighbouring

Bink Moss who stated that this area is among the top two or three moors in the north of England for the total of grouse shot during the season. The number of birds that the visitor sees and hears would seem to bear out that this was more than mere proprietorial boasting. The moor is certainly a model one and the young keeper a most efficient exponent of his art.

The red grouse *Lagopus scoticus* is unique in being the only endemic British bird – that is, it is not found outside the British Isles. The grouse only breed where there is heather for the young shoots of *calluna* are its staple food though it will also eat crowberry and cloudberry. This need for a continuous supply of the young plant has led to the burning of old heather on a regular rotation of a dozen to fifteen years and so, even on these remote moors, the vegetation has been modified and can hardly be called natural. The heather may be burned between October 1 and April 15 and the keeper has to choose his day well: too wet and the old heather will not burn, too dry and the underlying peat may catch alight. The burning is best done in small patches or strips so that there is a mixture of different ages of the plant in the same vicinity. Longer heather provides more protection for the hen and her eggs and chicks during the nesting season which coincides with the end of burning. Nearly a million acres of England are covered in grouse moors and the sport is economically very significant in many areas. Unfortunately its increasing importance is to the detriment of some moorland where new tracks have been bulldozed on to the fells to ease access for the vehicles which transport these sportsmen who seem to have forgotten how to walk.

Approaching the fell along the path to Hagworm Hill there is little evidence of any crag and, after initial dampness around the head of Hargill Beck, progress is easy. Incidentally, the Ordnance map appears to show the beck's main feeder as running uphill! Perhaps the surveyors were in a hurry to get away from the area as hagworm is a northern name for an adder.

There is a cairn at the top of the first, short climb and then, as Whernside comes into view far away to the south, the walking becomes a delight over a gently tilted plateau covered with very low heather through which protrude scattered stones. On crossing to the northern edge, the Long Crags themselves become apparent but they are more a line of boulders and scree than true crags. The view of upper Teesdale is very fine from the edge with Cow Green Reservoir dominating the valley. How much finer though had it not been built and had the Tees been allowed to continue to meander murkily through The Weel!

A line of "Shelled Area You Pass Here At Your Own Risk" signs is passed and the summit cairn found in the middle of a broad area of heather. The top is overawed by Mickle Fell and, although a bit of the Lake District can be spied through a gap in the Pennines and Great Dun Fell and Cross Fell are in sight, the flat nature of the summit area detracts from the view. Most walkers will probably have their hearts set on climbing Mickle Fell anyway and will not be wishing to linger on Long Crag.

There are patches of scree on the south side of the fell but these are not as prominent as the northern ones which have given the hill its name. To the south, in the Arngill Beck valley, lies Fish Lake, formerly Fish Pond, and a track leads down to meet the B6276 road a third of a mile east of Grains o' th' Beck. The track, a private road, services Close House Barytes Mine which is making its own contribution to the landscape. In time the scars will grass over and the remains will be looked at with interest by the few visitors who will come this way as evidence of the time when men forced a precarious living out of this wild country. The Ordnance Survey One-Inch sheet of 1867 shows that mining for lead was carried on at West Hush and East Hush close to the present mine.

Bink Moss

Bink Moss, 2,031 feet, according to the latest Ordnance Survey, is the the third and most easterly of the group of summits in the broad triangle of Yorkshire bounded by the Tees, the Lune and the county boundary. It is another grouse moor and is mostly heather-covered, though a line of low crags and boulders breaks the surface at Low Bink on the southern side. A fine cairn, standing by the path near Low Bink, was obviously constructed so as to be visible from Hagworm Hill at the head of Hargill Beck.

The summit is most easily visited from Hagworm Hill and a wire fence, mended in places with the ubiquitous binder twine, leads unerringly between the two. There are a couple of large shakeholes next to the fence and cloudberry grows in some profusion. *Rubus chamaemorus* is a member of the bramble family and is quite common on parts of the Pennines. Its fruit is edible and is rather like a large, hard raspberry which changes colour from red to almost yellow but with the accent always on shades of orange. The leaves are deciduous and in the autumn form a brown carpet under the heather. The first time I saw them I imagined that they must have been blown up from woodland somewhere down in the valley!

William T. Palmer, author of several books on walking a half century ago, was less than complimentary about the tops east of Mickle Fell: "A point 2028 feet is marked on Bink Moss, one at 2209 feet on Long Crags......Really these "tops" are part of Mickle Fell, and can scarcely be regarded as separate items." The visitor might well disagree, especially if all three tops are visited during the same walk. Palmer was using the original Ordnance Survey heights: the most recent maps show a three-foot increase.

Bink Moss's summit, marked by a cairn of three stones, is by a peaty tarn halfway between the fence corner and a stake. The view is interesting rather than dramatic but gives a good contrast between the bare slopes of Mickle Fell and the high Pennines on the one hand and the broadening Tees Valley stretching away to the south-east on the other. The northern scarp of the Cleveland Hills can be made out and smoke rises from the industries of Teesside. Indirectly it is these oil refineries, chemical plants and steel works which are responsible for the biggest change in the landscape in this area for centuries. The plan to construct Cow Green Reservoir, built to supply water to the developing industries, was pushed through in the face of opposition from botanists, conservationists and just about everyone else with any feeling for the countryside. Drowning an area rich in rare plants and with some industrial archaeological interest, but most importantly destroying for ever the unique tranquility of the upper Tees Valley, the reservoir was completed in 1971. The twentieth century's usual sop when something of inestimable damage has been perpetrated on the landscape was speedily provided and the visitor can now drive to the site and follow the nature trail.

Admirers of Wild Boar Fell 25 miles away to the south-west and one of the best mountains in the Pennines, though unfortunately just out of Yorkshire, will delight in its particularly sharply etched millstone grit cap as seen from this direction. Some would argue that this is all the justification needed for climbing Bink Moss.

As well as the right-of-way following the valley of Hargill Beck to the west of

Bink Moss, there is a bridlepath on the eastern side. This leaves the Pennine Way just beyond Wythes Hill and heads towards Holwick. A continuation of the fence over the top of Bink Moss crosses the path. Whichever route is followed, the walker is certain of the company of the grouse with their oft-repeated warnings against trespass. There are butts on all sides of the hill and Land-rover tracks have been made to cabins on the southern slopes.

I met the keeper up here with his dogs and gun doing the rounds on one bright, early April morning. He was surprised to find that anyone would come to these moors just for the walking, explaining that he had to tramp the fell every day. I explained that I'd come up from Woverhampton and that seemed to satisfy him.

Were Yorkshire's boundary to be followed southwards for twenty miles or so from Mickle Fell, or about half of that as the curlew flies, some extremely rough country would have to be crossed before the next 2,000-footer was reached.

White Mossy Hill

White Mossy Hill, 2,150 feet, stands where the boundary takes a ninety-degree change in direction. The line is rather contrary hereabouts for although it crosses White Mossy Hill's top it ignores the higher and more interesting top of Nine Standards Rigg which, although also lying on the watershed, remains firmly in Westmorland, or Cumbria, if you prefer. This was not always the case for the boundary once passed through the Nine Standards. Its straightened course across Ravenseat Moor away to the east seems to indicate the work of some former boundary commissioner.

It seems unlikely that anyone would climb White Mossy Hill without visiting the Standards or without taking advantage, on a clear day, of the view indicator erected to commemorate the wedding of Prince Charles and Lady Diana Spencer, in July, 1981.

The purist who wishes to ascend White Mossy Hill rather than descend to it from Nine Standards Rigg will probably approach from near the county boundary sign on the B6270 Keld-Kirkby Stephen road. This involves the crossing of Lamps Moss, an ill-drained area of peat and rushes whence water trickles eastwards to join the Swale or westwards into the Eden. Near this spot, in 1664, a packman was murdered and his body flung into one of the shake holes, Blue John Holes, which are north of the Road. No one was ever brought to justice for John Smith's murder, a ghastly event in this peaceful place.

The summit itself also stands on the watershed of northern England and it is interesting to speculate that on a wet day the rain draining from the right boot might end up in the North Sea while that oozing out of the left one may be destined for the Irish Sea. A cairn comprising two fairly hefty chunks of stone marks the summit which unfortunately is unlike any preconceived idea of what a watershed should be like and is certainly not designed for the rapid shedding of water.

The hill is named from the cotton grass which flourishes on its slopes. The name element *white* is a common one in the Pennines, from Derbyshire to Durham, and is indicative, through reference to the plant, of ill-drained ground. Two members of the family grow in wet, acid soil: *Eriophorum angustifolium* is the common, many-headed cotton-grass and *Eriophorum vaginatum*, otherwise known as hares tail grass, has a single tuft of the white, downy fruiting head. The plant fruits in May and June though the white heads continue to grace the moors for a further couple of months. Part of White Mossy Hill's western slopes are known as Black Hill, showing that cotton grass and peat are pretty inseparable. An outcrop of gritstone above Black Hill is given the name Coldbergh Edge and this is sometimes applied to the fell as a whole.

White Mossy Hill now sees many more visitors than formerly as it lies on the route of Alfred Wainright's delightful 'Coast to Coast Walk' between St. Bees Head and Robin Hood's Bay. The way leads up from Kirkby Stephen and over Hartley Fell before curving round to reach the Nine Standards. A walk of less than a mile over the Rigg brings the traveller to White Mossy Hill. A descent along the top of Coldbergh Edge, passing a fine cairn at Millstones, soon reaches the track alongside Ney Gill near a shooting cabin and a line of grouse butts. Once a pack-horse road, this is a right-of-way connecting the B6270 with the farm of Ravenseat in Whitsundale.

This area, to the south-east of White Mossy Hill's summit and bounded by the road and dale, is full of interest. Birkdale Tarn, visible from the summit, looks rather out of place lying as it does on a hilltop, but it must be remembered that it was artificially enlarged to provide water power for the Loanin End Lead Mine which stood by the confluence of Great Sleddale and Birkdale Becks. Standing by the tarn, surrounded by a great sweep of fells, the scale seems better. In some places it has a slabby or stony beach while elsewhere there are two-yard-high peaty cliffs, or little peaty coves rimmed with the scraps of heather stalks. There is even sand along some stretches of the tarn edge while the dam at its southern end is made of huge stone slabs. The tarn is little visited by people now, but it is usually haunted by curlew and is a breeding ground of gulls in season. On one Bank Holiday Monday when Swaledale was seething and the Tan Hill Inn was overflowing there was just a solitary gull bobbing in the middle of the tarn to keep me company.

Nearby is Hill Top Quarry which provided much of the stone used in building the lead mines and mills as well as local farms and barns. It is being worked again and the lovely honey colour of the freshly exposed stone contrasts with the greys of the weathered rock. Threepence a cartload was what farmers paid for the stone for the walls built to enclose the moors. The gritstone occurs in layers of different thicknesses and so stone from the quarry was suitable for constructing all parts of a building from thick slabs for lintels, sills and doorsteps to the thin slates for the roof. The modern fashion for the cladding and roofing of new buildings in traditional style must account for the welcome renaissance of the quarry.

If the minor road past the quarry entrance is followed down into Whitsundale, the secluded farm of Ravenseat will be reached after a mile or so. It was once a hamlet of ten or so families with an inn and a chapel and many of the menfolk worked in the coal mines at Tan Hill to the north-east. The old track between Ravenseat and the mines, crossing Robert's Seat, is difficult to follow in places now but the pack-horse bridge across Whitsundale Beck still remains to show the former importance of the route. In 1788, Ravenseat was described as a 'village', and two years later £50 was spent on repairing the track, described as a 'Pack and Prime Way from Kirkby Stephen to Barnard Castle'. So many of our hill tracks are pathways through time as well as place.

3
Hills O'Lead

Stonesdale Beck and Arkle Beck, two important tributaries of the Swale, rise on the wide, wild moorland in the vicinity of Tan Hill, where the highest inn in England greets weary Pennine Wayfarers as it has greeted miners, shepherds, jaggers and drovers for centuries past. A local story tells of one landlord going to renew his licence at Richmond. He had left the magistrate's court before he realised that no licensing hours had been mentioned. Straight away he returned only to be told that he had permission to stay open day and night – "Refuse no

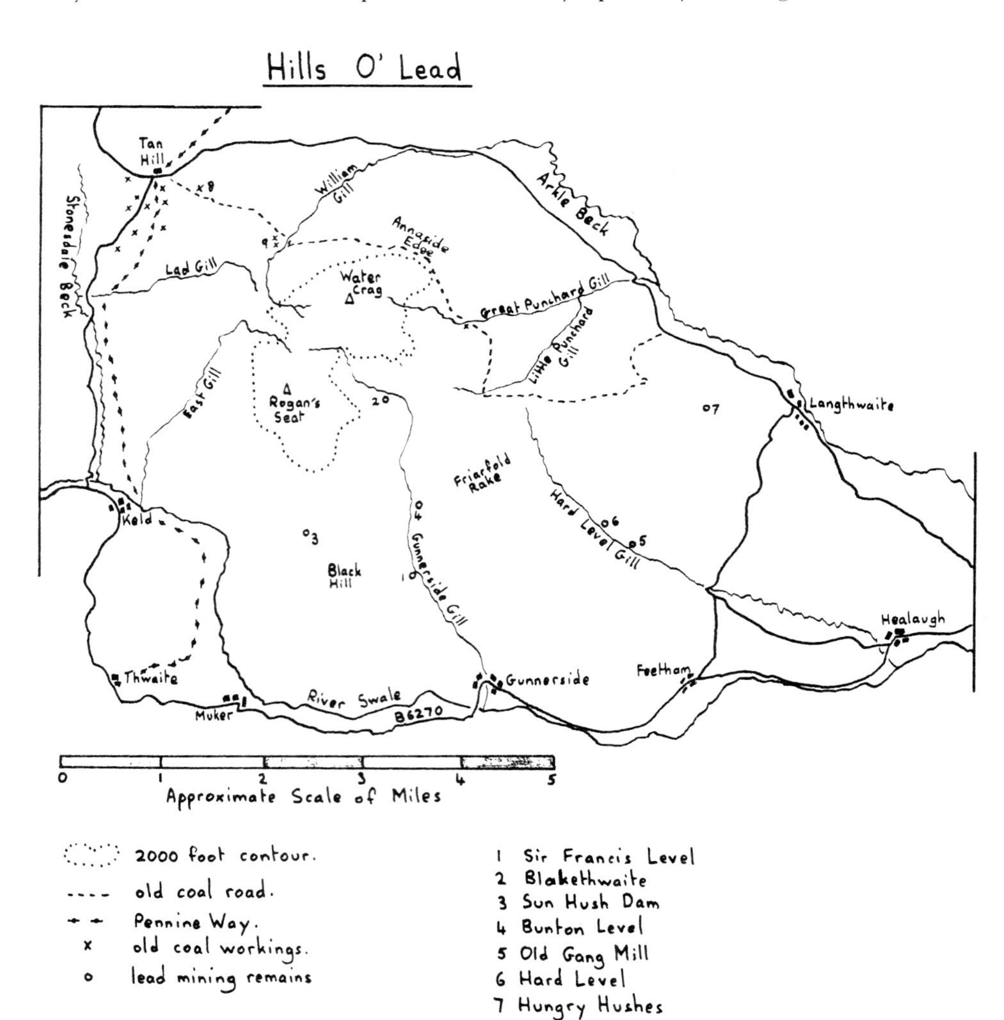

one at Tan Hill." We were glad to find this principle still being applied in August 1975 when we were walking the Pennine Way. After the long trek over Great Shunner Fell and Stonesdale Moor, a late afternoon beer was most welcome. This was in the days before licensing hours were liberalised. On enquiring what was in the pies in a glass case on the bar, a visitor was bluntly told: "Sheep. What else do you expect round here?"

The inn has been much altered recently but it is still an oasis on these bleak moors. There is always a welcoming fire and Pennine Wayfarers and others are invited to camp provided they replace stones and don't light fires for, after all, as the note in the bar says, "It's Free." There is also more on the menu now than sheep pies.

Between here and Swaledale, the land swells and rises, culminating in the two summits of Rogan's Seat and Water Crag. This is uncompromising country and the going, on the northern side of the fells at least, is as difficult as anything found in the county. Approaches from the south are rather easier in surroundings dominated by the remains of the lead mining industry which was the major economic force here from Elizabeth's reign to Victoria's.

Rogan's Seat

Rogan's Seat, 2,205 feet, is one of four two-thousanders in Yorkshire with this suffix. *Saetr* is an old Norse word signifying a summer pasture or the shieling *(saeter)* which was the temporary home of the folk looking after the livestock. Who Rogan was history does not tell, but the whole area resounds with words harking back to the Norsemen who settled these *dalr* and *fjalls* in the ninth and tenth centuries. Rogan may have worked closely with Gunnar who also had pasturage on the fell and after whom the settlement to the south, Gunnerside, was named. Perhaps they climbed the gills and followed the becks together, got water from the springs after which Keld is named and admired the waterfalls which we still call forces. Maybe they helped their fellow farmers to make the clearings which are recalled in the names of Thwaite and Blakethwaite and perhaps their descendants lent a hand when the soil was broken at Muker – the narrow, newly cultivated land – a name strongly suggestive of population pressures leading to the development of new settlements.

The area might have seen its first flowering during the days of the Norse settlement but it reached its prime with the development of the lead mines and the remains of the industry bite deeply into the flanks of both Rogan's Seat and Water Crag. If the walker wishes to gain an appreciation of the scope and extent of the former workings, then the approach to Rogan's Seat from the south can hardly be bettered, especially if Gunnerside is the starting point.

A quiet village now, Gunnerside's large Methodist chapel and former Mechanic's Institute indicate that it wasn't always the case. Like all the villages and hamlets in Swaledale, it has seen a decline in population since the peak of the industry in the middle of the nineteenth century. The parish of Melbecks, which includes Gunnerside, had a population of 1,274 in 1801 and this peaked at 1,661 in 1851. By 1891 it had fallen to 600 and in 1951 was less than 400. The 1981 figure of 282 souls shows a further decline and if the trend continues, the village's population will probably soon reach the level it was at a few generations after Gunnar settled here. Nowadays, though, the incomers are only part-time, buying cottages as second homes – a new kind of *saeter*.

A track leads up the east side of Gunnerside Gill and the first major mining site is reached within a mile where the remains of the Sir Francis Level crushing mill stands roofless on the flats by the beck. This long level was the culmination of mining in Gunnerside Gill and it was designed to reach new, deeper ground in the Friarfold and Blakethwaite areas. The work began in 1864, a last throw to try and exploit ores which were previously unworkable because they were too deep, and in order to reach the right depth it had to be driven in from 1,500 yards down the gill.

Five years after commencement the level had advanced 400 yards at a cost of five pounds a yard. Four men, working two six-hour shifts a day, had progressed at the rate of ten feet per month. Compressed air drills and later dynamite speeded up operations and the vein was cut in March 1877.

The workings associated with Sir Francis Level produced good ore and one of the companies involved, the A.D., is reckoned to have drawn £32,000 worth of ore up to 1880. This was to be the last success, for in 1882 the price of lead fell and work at the Gunnerside mines virtually ceased. The underground hydraulic pumping engine installed at a cost of £4,500 the previous year and which, being fed by water through cast-iron pipes from the Sun Hush Dam developed 50 horsepower, stopped working and never turned again.

Further up the gill the remains are most impressive, for the valley sides have been hacked about in an awesome way. This is especially so where the Bunton (or Bunting) Level is passed in an area scarred and mauled through centuries of working. Driven into the Old Rake Vein and entering the Friarfold Vein, the output from the level was very great, as is testified by the great piles of spoil from the dressing floors at the level mouth. At first the dressed ore was carried over the moors to be smelted at the Old Gang works in the next valley, Mill Gill, but Bunton had always been designed as an underground link to the neighbouring Hard Level complex and the breakthrough was made in 1828, though unfortunately not without difficulty. The agent responsible for the level, John Davies, managed to drive it at too high an angle which meant that an eight-yard shaft had to be sunk down on to Hard Level in order to join the two networks.

For the rest of the mine's working life, ore had to be tipped down into hoppers and then trammed out of Hard Level. Much of the ore from the Sir Francis Level made this long underground journey.

Most spectacular of all the relics associated with former land mining are the hushes and they abound in the middle reaches of Gunnerside Gill. A hush was firstly a way of proving the position of a vein of ore and sometimes a way of working it. It must have been one of the most spectacular sights in the lead Dales and the results are still dramatic after a couple of centuries. A dam was built high above the valley side and, when enough water had been impounded, it was breached, sending the flood roaring and scouring down the hillside, tearing away turf, soil and loose rock and exposing the bedrock, and hopefully the veins of galena, beneath. The technique was not always successful – Hungry Hushes above Arkengarthdale were supposed to have missed the vein, hence the name. The steep sides of Gunnerside Gill were ideal for hushing and where the Friarfold lead vein crosses the valley the sides are deeply etched and scored. The depth of some of these gullies are such as to suggest that they were hushed more than once. Redundant hushes are not of a great deal of use nowadays but they make ideal courses for trials motor cyclists and lines of little red flags are sometimes seen marking a route.

At the head of Gunnerside Gill are the remains of the Blakethwaite smelt mill. The Blakethwaite mine was a very old one and there are many old shafts and bell pits in the vicinity. The mill, one of the remotest in the Dales being only a little over a mile from the summit of Rogan's Seat, remained in use until 1878. It has suffered greatly from vandalism in recent years, a fate shared by many of our most important industrial monuments. Vandalism can be of the loutish variety but it can also have a more insidious nature: the vandalism by neglect as perpetrated by those who ought to know better. We seem to be exchanging our real heritage for packaged, artificial 'experiences'.

If Blakethwaite Gill is followed up to its source at Wham Bottom, a walk of about half a mile will lead to the top of Rogan's Seat.

The sheer number of routes from the south, particularly in and above Gunnerside Gill, demonstrate the former importance of the area which is criss-crossed by tracks and miner's paths. One which forsakes the valleys and makes an ideal and natural line of ascent for Rogan's Seat follows the broad spur of high land rising up above Gunnerside. As it climbs to Knot Top it crosses a bridlepath, now a made way to the butts higher up, and then goes over Black Hill with the aid of the odd sheep track and water cut. Cloudberry grows in great profusion on this part of the hill. To the west is Moss Dam, built to provide a head of water for a hydraulic engine in the Blakethwaite mine. Rogan's Seat is not a very striking looking hill but is least dumpy when seen from Black Hill. The view is marred by the bulldozed road leaving the right of way and heading for the summit. There is a 'No Access' sign at the foot of the road but that presumably refers to vehicles? It leads unerringly onwards, past grouse butts, up and over the summit. The purist can walk in the heather, two yards away from the track and parallel with it. I would prefer that there wasn't a road so as to be spared the dilemma!

The summit of Rogan's Seat is in the last throes of peat erosion. One or two dark brown hillocks protrude above the general plateau level but for the most part a good yard of the stuff has been stripped away to reveal the underlying surface which is now covered with grass interspersed with gritstone blocks. A theodolite would be needed to prove the summit and two cairns attempt to claim the distinction. One is perched on a peat hag and so will inevitably be forced eventually to recognise the claim of the other, thirty yards away, which sits on more secure foundations.

The direct approach to the top from Tan Hill to the north is difficult and seems long. Use can be made of an old pit track to the vicinity of West Grain but then all is heathery floundering until the grouse road is met just north-west of the summit plateau. It is easier to visit neighbouring Water Crag first.

Water Crag

Water Crag, 2,192 feet, stands just over a mile north-east of Rogan's Seat. As a descriptive name it is at least half correct for it is the birthplace of many streams. The crag is confined to a short stretch on the north-western edge of the summit plateau. Most of the streams draining off Water Crag's benevolent flanks find their way, eventually, into the Swale by way of William Gill, Great Punchard Gill, Gunnerside Gill and East Gill, though the north-western corner of the hill is drained by Mirk Fell Gill which flows into the Greta and thence into the Tees.

The popular guidebook author, William Palmer, writing in the late thirties was less than complimentary about this area. "These are little visited hills in empty moors, the only paths being to disused mines. They are not cheerful places at the best, and miserable and difficult in poor weather and outside the summer season." There may be a certain cheerlessness about the fells here but there is also a stark beauty in the rolling, open skyline and the blue distance of the horizon while the lack of visitors is a positive part of their attraction. I daresay a hundred folk pass through the bar of the Tan Hill Inn for every one who ventures onto Water Crag.

A bridleway crosses the fell's north-eastern slopes, running roughly parallel with the road from Tan Hill to Reeth which it predates and which became the turnpike in 1770. It lies about a mile from the road and is about 600 feet above it. This was a coal road which linked the Tan Hill pits to the lead smelters. To the modern eye the area around Tan Hill looks an unlikely industrial setting but coal mining was important for six centuries. There are still over a hundred disused pits, shafts and levels marked on the Ordnance map within a mile of the inn. At this western end the coal road is not easy to find or follow but it is well worth the effort to try.

Leaving the tarred road 200 yards east of the inn it makes first for the King's Pit Colliery which is known to have been working in the seventeenth century. Here is a small pool and the remains of a rectangular building. Crossing Mirk Fell Edge, where it is marked by cairns, the track continues to an area of old bell pits around the head of William Gill. A line of boundary stones running along Mirk Fell Edge have a large letter B picked out in white paint on their eastern sides. William Gill Houses show some substantial remains and the track running beside the beck from its foot at the road is a far easier approach to Water Crag than the bridleway from Tan Hill.

The best section of the coal road, a firm green ledge on the hillside, now contours round Annaside Edge and West Moor, marked by some fine cairns, before dropping down to Great Punchard Gill at another coal mine, this time exploited by a level. This small concern was on the eastern boundary of the small Tan Hill coal field and besides the level, which has run in a few yards from the entrance, there are the scant remains of a rectangular building and a bridge. On one visit, a shaft had crowned in higher up the hillside exposing a circular masonry lining with water thirty odd feet down. While such a shaft remains open it is a great danger to sheep. There are several other workings in the vicinity of Great and Little Punchard Gills and the mineral which was exploited can be identified by the colour of the spoil; grey shale indicating a coal mine while a paler spoil shows that lead was worked.

The track bifurcates just east of Great Punchard Head with the clearer branch running down Great Punchard Gill and over Whaw Moor to join the road through Arkengarthdale. The other path goes southwards across Little Punchard Head and Friarfold Moor where it crosses the line of the Friarfold lead vein. The course of the latter can be clearly followed for nearly three miles between Gunnerside Gill and Hungry Hushes because of the disturbance to the ground which has taken place. Spoil heaps, hushes, bell pits and rakes leave a pale scar on the ground which is visible from Great Shunner Fell, on the far side of Swaledale. Half a mile south of Friarfold Rake the path crosses the main track between Gunnerside Gill and Mill Gill and enters an area criss-crossed with a multiplicity of paths and tracks, all of which are worth exploring.

The old coal road can be left anywhere along Annaside Edge and a way made across the heather to a small but prominent cairn at 933048 on the map. The cairn does not mark the summit but is a good example of a shepherd's mark standing on the plateau edge where it will be most easily visible. Another fine cairn, Standard Man, stands tall a mile and a third to the east. The actual summit is marked by a trig point (OSBM2963) with a substantial and effective shelter nearby. Presumably the Ordnance Survey chose Water Crag for its column rather than the higher (by thirteen feet!) top of Rogan's Seat because of the former's more central position in the area. To the west of the summit is a cairn built like a short wall, or a wall built like a stout cairn, five feet high and six long. Further west again, a wire fence marks the way south-westwards towards Rogan's Seat.

The trig point gives good views across to Great Shunner Fell and the back of the Mallerstang ridge while the Nine Standards stand out so clearly that they can be counted away to the north-west. The line of the old Roman road over Stainmore is picked out by the green fields below it and the moor above. On one sunny morning a row of sparkling beads, like dew on a cobweb, was slowly moving along it, cars and lorries reflecting the sun as they toiled across the A66. Beyond Stainmore Mickle Fell broods in its peaty fastness and, further round to the east, the white-painted farms of upper Teesdale can be seen.

That rather rare member of the linnet family, the twite, a small, brown bird, nests on Water Crag but the visitor is more likely to meet that companion of the moors, the red grouse, especially on the northern side of the hill where there are several lines of butts. Still in the avian world, the area south-west of the summit and lying just behind the actual line of Water Crag bears the place-name Moor Hen Nest. The last time I was by the trig point a pair of dunlin fussed and scurried about, scouring the heather for insects.

4
On Mallerstang Edge

Mallerstang is the north-south valley chosen by the Midland Railway when it built its adventurous Settle-Carlisle extension between 1869 and 1872. Spawning the sources of the Eden and Ure the valley was the logical, indeed probably the only, choice, and at Aisgill the track reaches its summit of 1,169 feet. Williams *Midland Railway* of 1877 describes it as "a very narrow constricted valley... ..along which in winter the wind sweeps with bitter blasts" while another Victorian author commenting on the line and its environs states that: "Mallerstang ...will often call forth the admiration of the railway traveller. Baugh Fell, Wild Boar Fell, Lunds Fell and High Seat, with their compeers, will always, when free from mists, form an exquisite mountain landscape." An important element in this landscape is the line of craggy, gritstone outcrops, breaking the slopes between 1,750 and 2,000 feet, which emphasises the shape and line of Mallerstang Edge like a rocky bulwark.

The valley had long been a direct route between the Dales and the Eden Valley before the advent of the railway and it is not surprising that the remains of two castles, Pendragon and Lammerside, guard its northern reaches. Some places shrug off the passage of time and bear the marks of human endeavour through the centuries, the broken remains of castles, the miles of enclosure walls and the snaking railway, in a way which seems ageless.

The Yorkshire boundary follows the eastern edge of the valley of Mallerstang for four miles from Lamps Moss to where it plunges down to the valley floor in the company of Hell Gill Beck. Three summits top two thousand feet along the boundary and a further one stands completely in the county a mile to the south.

Mallerstang is a fine-sounding name and is probably derived from a combination of the primitive Cumbric *mel,* meaning bald or bare, and the old Norse *stong,* a boundary mark or pole. A bare-topped hill marking a boundary certainly seems a more credible explanation than the Mallard's Stank (wild duck pool) favoured by some writers, for the latter sounds like an etymological wild duck chase!

High Seat

High Seat, 2,326 feet, is the most northerly 2,000-footer along the ridge if the claim of High Pike Hill for separate status is ignored. From Lamps Moss on the B6270 road which threads its way from Swaledale to the Eden Valley, High Pike Hill looks quite commanding but on gaining the top it is seen to be a sham and merely the northern end of a gently rising slope which culminates on High Seat. This northern approach to High Seat is a satisfying and natural line as it follows the watershed. It also has the advantage of starting at an altitude of 1,698 feet.

The walk leaves the road near the county boundary with Westmorland, now Cumbria, and it is better to use the green track which starts on the far side of the boundary, for to attempt to follow the line exactly will only result in crossing the wettest part of the moss. The escarpment is quite steep and affords plenty of opportunities for stopping for retrospective glances across to White Mossy Hill and Nine Standards Rigg.

The top of High Pike Hill is marked by a cairn and then the way forward crosses a slightly tilted plateau for more than a mile before High Seat is reached. On a really clear day, though, the walker may get no further than High Pike Hill for the view from the top is outstanding, encompassing the Lakeland fells, the high Pennines around Cross Fell, the Howgill fells, Nine Standards Rigg, Wild Boar Fell and Rogan's Seat as well as the Tan Hill Inn.

The peat has been virtually blown away in the slight depression between the tops, a sure indicator of the force and route of the prevailing wind and there are large areas with scant vegetation and patches of stony ground. The scouring has occurred less and the peat is thicker higher up. On the east side of High Pike Hill is Uldale Gill Head, usually taken to be the source of the Swale, although that name is not adopted for another five miles, at the confluence of Birkdale Beck and Great Sleddale Beck. The ridge of which High Seat is the summit is the birthplace of three major rivers, for the Ure and Eden also rise on this, the watershed of England, and standing on the boundary there is but one county between here and the sea on either side.

Apart from in the vicinity of High Seat's summit there is little semblance of a path along this northern part of the ridge although a very important sheep track is crossed halfway between High Pike Hill and the top. Some people disparage sheep but in their own domain they are not stupid. Their tracks are always well graded and are heading somewhere important, for sheep at least, like a prominent boulder or scratching post. Many is the time when this writer has been thankful for the path creation carried out by hundreds of dainty feet.

The highest point is not marked but there is a cairn on both sides of it. The view is better from the northern cairn, with the Yorkshire hills looking especially striking and stretching away to fold after fold of fell like some mighty, crumpled, grey-green counterpane. Great Shunner Fell displays its vastness while Rogan's Seat lumbers above the blue glint of Birkdale Tarn. Human striving is put into scale on these lonely heights for there are few obvious marks of activity and to spend an hour in this wild and lonely loveliness is to experience a broadening of the mind and a cleansing of the soul.

A shorter, but steeper route to the top follows a right-of-way which zig-zags up the fellside from the hamlet of Outhgill to the vicinity of Mallerstang Edge.

In the hamlet is a replica of the Jew Stone, first erected by William Mounsey to commemorate his 1850 walk from the Eden's mouth to its source. The original stone stood on the fellside but was broken during the construction of the railway. The track was built to serve the old coal pits which exploited the local thin seams in the days before the railway brought better quality fuel to the area.

The upper stages of this route give a more intimate appreciation of the gritstone crags than do other approaches and indeed their presence is totally unsuspected from the summit although the equivalent line of crags can be seen across the valley on Wild Boar Fell. After savouring the summit solitude on High Seat most walkers will wish to continue southwards along the watershed and the next 2,000-foot top is reached after half a mile or so of easy going.

Archy Styrigg

2,280 feet, is so named on the six-inch map where its summit is called Gregory Chapel. These are fine names but surely more appropriate to a nineteen-thirties murder mystery than a fell top: Gregory, the dashing second son of some cinctured earl, and his sidekick, the ever faithful, though rather naive Archy. We can see the latter most at home with practicalities: engines, wiring diagrams and footslogging whilst Gregory pursues the more cerebral problems of solving society murders......"Good man, Archy!" exclaimed Gregory. "Oh, I say, do you mean that, Greg? Thanks awfully."

Sty means a steep place, or more usually the way up one, while *Rigg* refers to a ridge. *Archy* may well be a personal name but from a while further back than the nineteen-thirties. A path does climb steeply up behind Outhgill but it heads more towards High Seat. Perhaps Gregory came up here to seek calm and inspiration. If so, he was certainly a fine judge. The fell is often named Mallerstang Edge because that is the name shown nearest to the summit on most of the popular maps but this is really a misnomer for the Edge is a definite feature of the western slopes rather than the tops. The summit has gained 30 feet thanks to the resurvey which the O.S. carried out during the 1970s, for on previous maps the height was shown as being just over 2,250 feet.

Archy Styrigg is separated from High Seat by Brockholes Gill and Outhgill and from its southerly neighbour, Hugh Seat, by Red Gill and the headwaters of

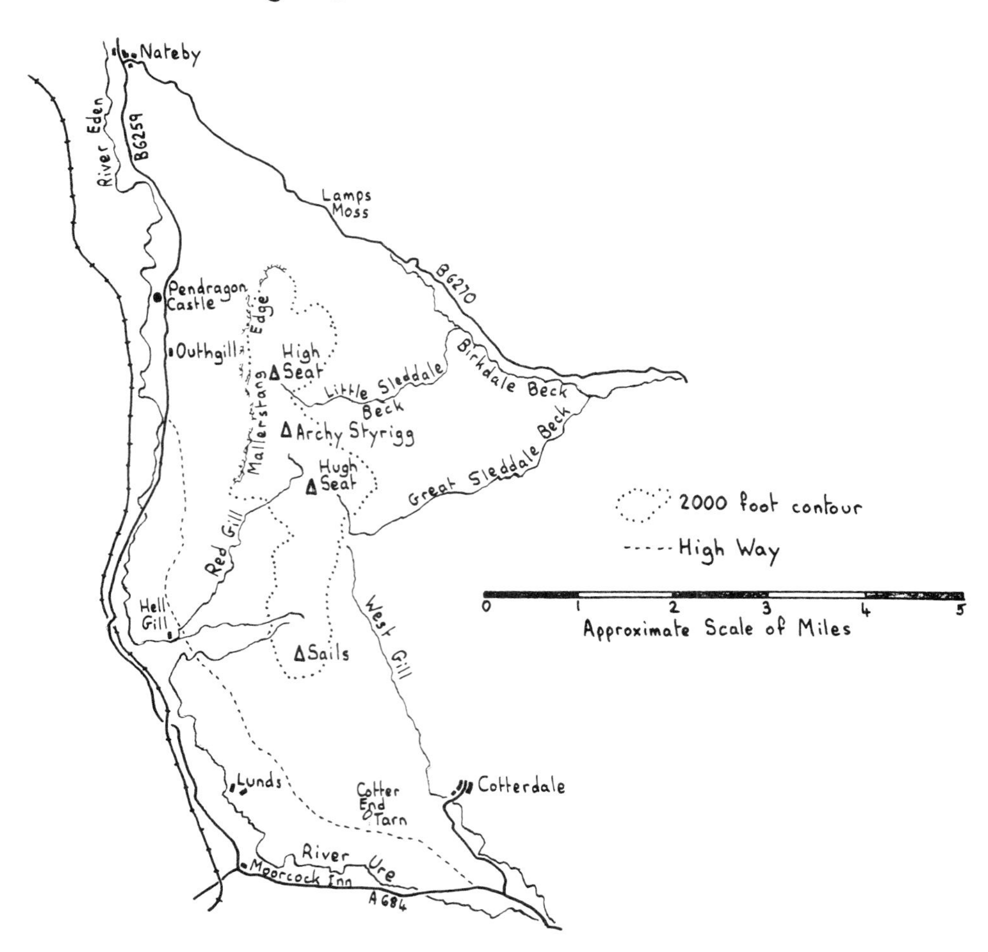

Great Sleddale Beck. The summit is marked by a small pile of stones while there is a more prominent cairn a hundred yards further south. This is another wide and flat grassy top and one which steadfastly refuses to take seriously its location on the main watershed of northern England.

The walker who has reached thus far will be pleased to be able to contradict Daniel Defoe's description of "the hills of Mallerstang Forest, which are, in many places, unpassable". The view south is good with Great Knoutberry Hill and Whernside acting as a frame for the unmistakable table top of Ingleborough. The summit is near enough to the Edge to provide glimpses of the Eden Valley and the sandwich cake composition of Wild Board Fell thrusts up its bulk across Mallerstang.

The walking is easy here and the temptation to carry on is great for the next summit, Hugh Seat, is only a mile away. The broad ridge, and the watershed and the county boundary and the Yorkshire Dales National Park boundary and the parish boundary between Mallerstang and Muker, all of which follow it, changes direction on the top of Archy Styrigg and from running due south, it now trends south-east, heading in the direction of Great Shunner Fell and the heart of Yorkshire's big country.

A fine currack, as high as a man, is passed which overlooks the wastes of the gathering grounds of Little Sleddale Beck, home to curlew and grouse. At the broad col between Red Gill and Little Sled Dale, Archy Styrigg is left behind and a hill with a history is approached.

Hugh Seat

Hugh Seat, 2,257 feet, is one of many hills named after someone but one of the few where we know something about the person so honoured. Hugh de Morville was involved with the murder of Thomas à Becket in Canterbury Cathedral in December 1170. He was not implicated in the actual death but rather held back the crowds at the entrance to the transept who might have attempted to save the martyr. Such was the enmity which people felt towards the perpetrators of the crime that Hugh and his companions are said to have hidden for a year in his castle at Knaresborough. Later, as a result of Hugh's involvement in rebellion, the de Morville lands were forfeited to the crown but eventually were given back to the family. Hugh's sister, Maud, married into the de Veteripont family and a descendant, Lady Anne Clifford, who owned Pendragon Castle in the valley as well as those at Appleby, Brougham and Brough nearby, built the stone pillar which stands near the summit. It is inscribed AP 1664 on one side and FHL 1890 on the other.

The cairn was no doubt set up by Lady Anne, while she was staying at Pendragon, to mark the limits of her land. Indeed the fell top was known locally as Lady's Pillar. It was restored by a later lord of the manor, Captain Frederick Horner Lyell, hence the carving on the other face. Hugh Seat has appeared in the past under the different guises of Hugh's Seat, Hugh Seat Morville and Hucat Morville.

The summit, a rounded knoll rising above the general level of the ridge and visible from the valley, is marked with a cairn of half a dozen stones, a much less impressive feature than Lady Anne's hoary old boundary currack.

Hugh Seat is in a pivotal position on the watershed, with streams draining from its slopes into the Eden, Swale and Ure, a claim to fame unique amongst the Yorkshire fells, or any other, come to that. It is the birthplace of the River Eden though Daniel Defoe disputes this, stating that the river rises on "the side of a monstrous high mountain, called Mowill Hill, or Wildbore Fell, which you please"; but most other authorities take Hell Gill Beck, with its tributary Red Gill, to be the main source. There is always a sense of adventure in trying to trace a river to its origin but there is also a feeling of uncertainty. Which of the many tricklets which unite to form Red Gill Beck or any of Hell Gill Beck's feeders is the *real* headwater? Sources move according to the prevailing weather conditions. Water oozing from some peaty depression may be blown either way depending on the strength and direction of the wind. On a really wet day, if the source is taken to be the highest feeder and you happen to be standing on the watershed, then it may be the water dripping off the end of your nose. At least cairns and trig points don't move, though on a day of low cloud or hill fog the visitor might well imagine that they do!

Hell Gill is well worth exploring and can be used as a route of ascent for Hugh Seat. Its lower reaches are the best parts for it has been overdeepened and has cut itself a fine, half-hidden gorge. In former times, before glacial action disturbed matters, Hell Gill Beck flowed into the Ure and it still seems to be heading in that direction for the first couple of miles of its course. Moraine dumped at the end of the last ice age diverted the stream so that it now turns back on itself and flows north to form the Eden proper after its confluence with Ais Gill Beck. The drop down to Mallerstang is greater than the fall to the head of Wensleydale and so ever since the end of the last glaciation Hell Gill Beck has had to work hard, trying to cut down to the level of its adoptive river. The full reach of Hell Gill Gorge can only be explored by those willing to get very wet for a through journey from top to bottom is possible only by following the beck itself, at times down waterfalls six feet high and through narrow passages which are almost cave-like – an adventurous expedition for a hot, anticyclonic summer's day when visibility on the tops precludes a good view. It is difficult to get a good view of the gorge from its edge for trees growing alongside obscure the best portions, although a glimpse of its depths may be obtained from Hell Gill Bridge, just above the farm of the same name.

This old stone bridge used to carry the main road through Mallerstang, the High Way, until the present route was turnpiked in 1825. For a mile or so Hell Gill Beck forms the county boundary and it is said that Dick Turpin once leapt his horse across the gill to escape from the wrath of the Westmorland magistrates. The same tale is told of a more local highwayman, 'Swift Nick' Nevison, and unless leaping Hell Gill was some kind of regular sport for gentlemen of the road it seems likely that some confusion has arisen.

From Hugh Seat's summit there is a choice of routes. Cotterdale can be reached either by following West Gill or by descending the long tongue of Mid Rigg or a splendid and rewarding, though pathless and tough, way may be made, past Knoutberry currack, to Great Shunner Fell. Two miles south of Hugh Seat is the only top along the Mallerstang ridge to be wholly in Yorkshire.

Sails

Sails, 2,185 feet, is both the most southerly and the lowest of the Mallerstang Edge summits. Half a mile to the north, the top named Little Fell on the maps rises to a height of 2,188 feet and is thus the mathematical summit of the fell. The Ordnance Survey chose the slightly lower Sails for its ring trig point and this is certainly superior as a viewpoint. Its alternative name of Ure Head is more descriptive for the river rises in a peaty depression 500 yards north of the summit. This is a confusing area of peat groughs, confusing to the source seeker anyway, for not all the rain falling in this waste is destined for the North Sea. A drop or two finds its way westwards into the Irish Sea because tributaries of Hell Gill Beck also drain away from the dip between Sails and Hugh Seat. However, by far the majority of water falling on Sails finds its way into the Ure and this is unusual as so many Pennine fells lie on major or minor watersheds that their run-off is often fairly evenly split.

The Ure, which bears this name straight from its source, spends a couple of miles travelling westwards before correcting itself at Ure Crook and flowing east towards its true destination.

The ascent of Sails is an easy matter for it is simply a case of finding a suitable spot to leave the old High Way and striking up the fellside. There is no difficulty for the gritstone edge which is so much a feature of the more northern parts of Mallerstang is absent here. The Ure itself, or its tributary of Washer Gill, can be followed, both having carved little valleys for themselves in which the water slides and tumbles over and round little blocks of stone. They are chattering, lively mountain streams and are good companions on the ascent which is otherwise a dull walk over grassy sheepwalks. The slope, moreover, is a convex one and the walker does not see the target until high up on the hill. Concave slopes are open and honest, convex ones tend towards deceit and the best that can be said of them is that they get the steepest climbing over with first. A footpath crosses the southern ridge of Sails, known as Tarn Hill, between Cotterdale and High Dyke to give an alternative approach.

Sails is properly only the name of the summit, the fell itself having as many different designations as there are ways of looking at it. Abbotside Common, Bubble Hill, Tarn Hill, Thwaite Bridge Common, Lunds Fell, Little Fell, Ure Head and Cotter End are all to be found on the map. Abbotside Common is from the previous ownership of this large area, stretching from here to Lovely Seat, by the monks of Jervaulx Abbey, nearly 30 miles down Wensleydale. The brothers were interested in wool and this is still sheep farming land though some forestry has appeared in Cotterdale on the southern slopes. Tarn Hill comes from Cotter End Tarn which sits on a boggy shelf at 1,650 feet. Lunds Fell is derived from the little settlement in the valley south-west of the fell. It is said that a form of Norse dialect was spoken in these parts until the time of Elizabeth I and the whole area is certainly full of Scandinavian place-names. There are villages in Norway and Sweden called Lund which, like this Yorkshire version, come from *lundr,* a wood.

The summit is marked by an Ordnance Survey ring triangulation station and a small cairn. There are bigger and better ones in the vicinity. The panorama from the summit is wide-ranging with the Three Peaks etched sharply to the south, Great Shunner and Wild Boar fells dominating the near scene and, if you are lucky, a distant prospect of Scafell Pike. In the middle of such wild grandeur it seems odd to catch a glimpse of the settled market town of Hawes while the railway buildings of Aisgill and Garsdale Head look strangely out of place, escapees from a Victorian toy train set.

The High Way crosses the western and southern slopes of Sails at an altitude ranging from 1,300 feet by Hell Gill to 1,600 feet on Cotter End. Its local name of Streets indicates a Roman origin and even though the route was described by Lady Anne Clifford in the mid-seventeenth century as running "over Cotter and those dangerous ways", it was presumably the best way for a carriage until 1826 when the present road from Garsdale Head through Mallerstang was built. Mary Queen of Scots travelled the High Way in 1568 on her way to bleak Bolton Castle twenty miles down Wensleydale. The Way is now a splendid pedestrian route, much of it on springy turf along a limestone platform. High Dyke, presently in a ruinous state, was formerly an inn for drovers and jaggers and was used as such until 1877.

The walker who has followed the Mallerstang Edge ridge all the way from Lamps Moss, over High Seat, Archy Styrigg, Hugh Seat and Sails cannot have failed, if the weather has been kind, to have spent some time looking eastwards, across the wet gathering grounds of the Swale and Ure towards that most massive of Yorkshire hills, Great Shunner Fell.

5
The Big Country

Great Shunner Fell

Great Shunner Fell, 2,349 feet, lives up to its description in many ways. It stands in the largest area of Yorkshire devoid of roads, a 40-square mile chunk of land which also takes in the Mallerstang fells, and has the largest summit area over 2,000 feet of any Yorkshire mountain. This sprawling top, shaped like a barbed arrow pointing north-westwards, is 2½ miles from east to west and nearly two miles from north to south. It has the largest number of cairns and curracks in the county, some of them magnificent examples of construction and visible from miles around. Its summit is the highest point approached by the Pennine Way in over a hundred miles from Edale and it is the highest point on the Way in Yorkshire. The climb from the bridge over Fossdale Gill at Hardraw is the longest continuous ascent along the entire long-distance path if approached from the south, a five-mile trudge in bad weather but a pleasure if the day is fair. It is an easy climb with the fifteen hundred odd feet being gained painlessly and, on a bright, clear, crisp winter's morning, it is a delight for the senses as well as good exercise for the legs.

Viewed from neighbouring Lovely Seat and granted a fair amount of imagination, Great Shunner Fell's top has rather the aspect of a wedge of cheese: Wensleydale, of course, for the hill surveys all aspects of life in that beautiful valley. Mind, there is a little of the *Gruyère* about the Buttertubs, a collection of solution holes on the eastern slopes, near the top of the pass of the same name. This is the finest road between Wensleydale and Swaledale to the north, though

Winter majesty in Swaledale, with Great Shunner Fell in the background. (Geoffrey N. Wright)

no longer the challenge which it used to be in the early days of motor cycles and cars.

The Buttertubs exist because of the rocks, which round here belong to the Yoredale series. Given the former name for Wensleydale, where these rocks are seen to good advantage, the Yoredales exert a profound effect on much of the Yorkshire Dales landscape. They consist of alternating layers of limestone, sandstone and shale repeated cyclically and are often found sandwiched between the older Great Scar Limestone beneath and the younger millstone grit on top. A cap of resilient gritstone has given Great Shunner, Penyghent and several other Yorkshire fells, most notably Ingleborough, their summit plateaux.

The Yoredale rocks give the fellsides a stepped appearance through differential erosion but their effect does not stop there. When they break down, the rocks, because of their differing chemical composition, form varying soils and those developing on the sandstones and shales give rise to an acid soil encouraging the growth of plants which break down to form peat. It is tricklets of water draining from this sour soil which have eroded downwards to form the sculpted, columnar Buttertubs with their fluted sides.

The five Buttertubs lie athwart the road, just down from the pass summit on the Swaledale side. They are interconnected and joined by little limestone bridges. A local once described them as bottomless, but added that some were deeper than that. They are, in reality, about twenty yards deep and their bottoms are covered in rocks and pebbles thrown down by visitors.

Great Shunner Fell can be climbed from the top of the Buttertubs pass and this approach is guaranteed to be quiet and peaceful even when the Pennine Way is thronged. I walked up this way one August, over two miles of gently ascending grass and peat with areas of stones and sand like dried-up tarn beds, and had the company of nothing but sheep and curlew which wheeled and dived and uttered their plaintive rising call. An old wall marks the route for the first part of the climb but then it is just a matter of steering a course between the headwaters of streams which will eventually find their way into the Swale or Ure. The top of Little Shunner Fell is crossed on the way to the summit and a stretch of stone wall runs aslant across the slight depression between the two. Why the wall was built linking nowhere and nowhere, I could only ponder on.

On that warm, August afternoon, the summit and its crowds came as a shock which pulled me out of my lone reverie. A score or so of Wayfarers were sitting on the gritstone boulders of the cairn and they kept arriving and departing. The Pennine Way has certainly lost none of its attraction and it remains a great challenge even though it is now wearing a bit thin in parts. It was the inspiration of Tom Stephenson, a mighty walkers' champion, which got the idea off (or on to) the ground in the decades between his first suggestion of the idea in 1935 and the completion of the route in 1965. By the time the Wayfarer is on the summit of Great Shunner, seven or eight days from Edale, muscles are attuned to the effort, boots are comfortable and the urban mind has calmed to the pedestrian pace. And it's not even halfway!

An Ordnance Survey column carrying the number S7747 stands partly in the sandwich-strewn cairn which is situated at the northern end of the fell. Sheep do well here.

For all its broad girth and size, Great Shunner is less noticed in the landscape than other lower and more shapely tops and it does not even lie on the Pennine watershed: this runs along the edge above Mallerstang, a few miles to the west. The view from the top is wide-ranging rather than exciting, with high, rolling moorland stretching away in all directions: the name derives from a Norse word

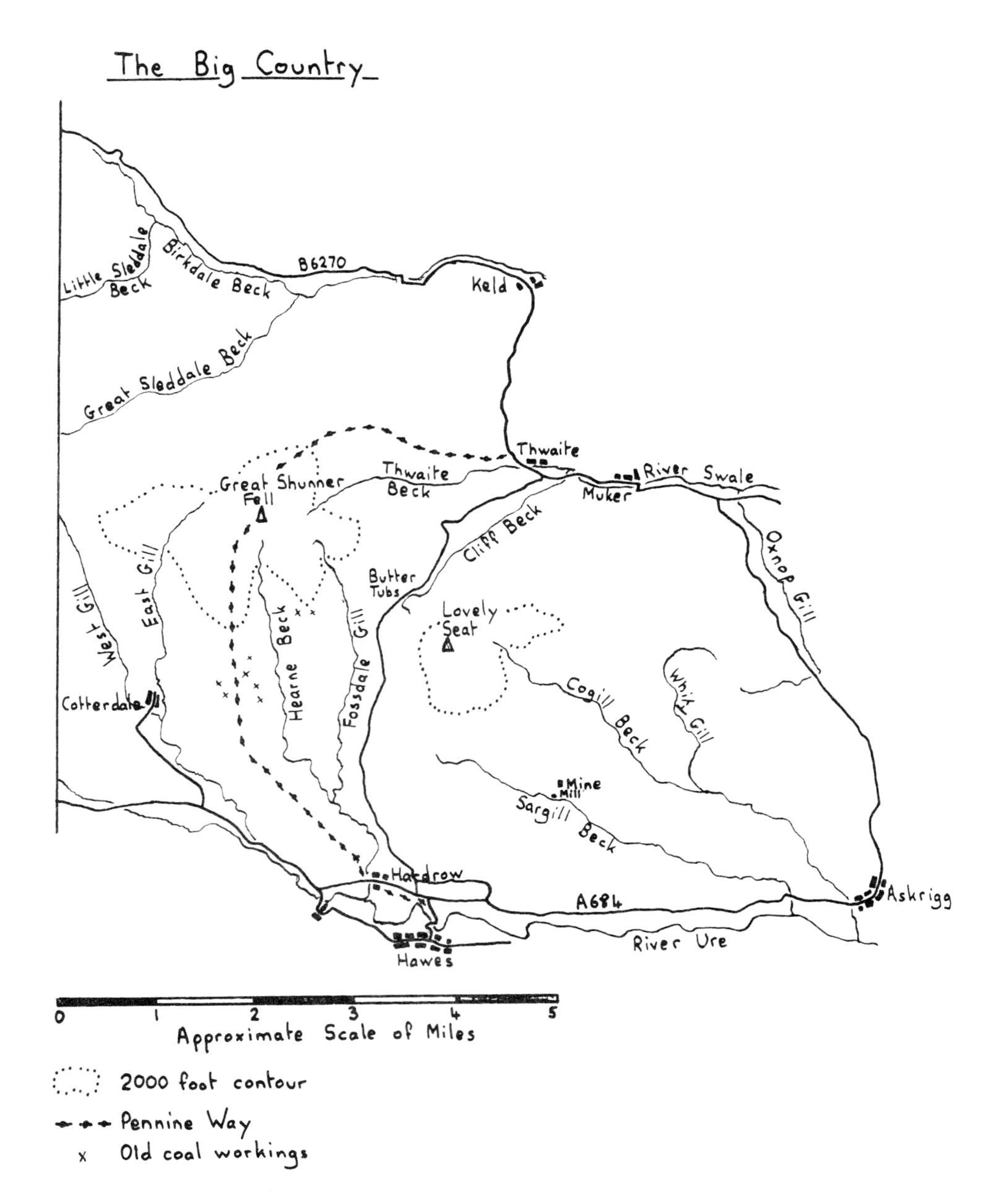

for a lookout hill. Whernside and Ingleborough stand out to the south, Mickle Fell is glanced northwards and the Lake District fells are glimpsed beyond Mallerstang. Pale scars and patches on Rogan's Seat, half a dozen miles to the north-east, are reminders of the lead mining which was so important in Swaledale until a century ago. The outlook is better from the higher slopes than from the cairn itself and there are grand views, on the descent, of the valleys to north or south. Swaledale, narrow and sinuous, contrasts with the broader, richer-looking Wensleydale.

Great Shunner Fell has been mined in the past. Indeed, the lower part of the track from Hardraw was built to serve the coal pits dotted over its southern slopes. One of these, on the east side of Cotterdale, was worked until well in to the twentieth century, supplying a large area with its domestic coal. The Pennine Way passes a large group of bell pits between Black Hill Moss and Bleak Haw. On the eastern slopes of the fell, below Pickersett Edge are two stone structures, having the shape of semi-circular walls supported in the middle by a buttress. Between the two, which are not aligned, is a depression, possibly the top of an old shaft. That these remains have a connection with the former coal industry is obvious but what that link was is not so clear. Possibly they formed parts of a shaft-top cover, rather like a Derbyshire lead miner's coe, or perhaps the walls were once part of the support for a primitive winding system. All of these pits worked outcrops of the Tan Hill coal, occuring between the top of the Yoredales and the base of the millstone grit.

In desolate Great Sled Dale, north of the summit, lie the remains of a copper mine which produced some ore. Local tradition speaks of large veins still waiting to be discovered but another story is probably nearer the truth. A speculator from Reeth employed two men on the mine and they struck a vein. One stayed to work the ore while the other went down the valley to tell the proprietor the good news. He had to walk the fourteen miles to Reeth and then the two men returned in a horse and cart. By the time they reached the mine the vein had been worked out.

Parts of Great Shunner Fell resemble the opposite of those biblical cities which were utterly destroyed to leave no stone standing on another. The cairn builders have been at work here for centuries and the hill is liberally endowed with examples of their art. The summit cairn is a hastily thrown together specimen but many others are finely built like the one on the end on Jinglemea Crag which is ten feet high and six across at the base. The Ordnance Survey uses the full width of its vocabulary to differentiate, in different places, between piles of stones, beacons, cairns and curracks. The finest group consists of well over a dozen, the best being six-footers, standing on Stony Edge, south-east of the summit near three tarns. Few, except Pennine Wayfarers locked in to their route, will be able to resist crossing to visit the colony of stone men and few, having reached them, will be able to resist adding a contribution.

As a change from the normal routes of ascent, following the Pennine Way from Hardraw or Thwaite, a Cotterdale horseshoe round can be followed. This zig-zags up East Side, passing the old Cotterdale coal pit, to join the Pennine Way below the Jinglemea Crag beacon, and following the Way to the summit. From there the direction is westwards, past Knoutberry Currack and across the broad, peaty neck of land which descends to the wet depression where rise northwards-flowing Great Sleddale Beck and southbound West Gill.

A little further, on the southern slopes of Hugh Seat, rise streams which join the Swale, Ure and Eden. The route turns southwards, over the summit of Sails, then down over Bubble Hill to Tarn Hill and the path back down to Cotterdale. This is a fine walk of ten or so miles with definite contrasts between the easy going of the Pennine Way and the tough crossing of the ridge from Great Shunner to Mallerstang. On the first leg of the walk there will almost certainly be company but after the summit of Shunner Fell it is unlikely that any other person will be seen until Cotterdale is reached again.

In the unlikely event of Great Shunner Fell being too small to find that solitude which is one of the most glorious features of the Yorkshire fells, then the walker has only to cross the top of the Buttertubs pass and climb the hill with one of the most attractive names in the county, where seclusion is virtually guaranteed.

Swaledale, with Great Shunner Fell in the centre distance and Muker village in the valley. (Geoffrey N. Wright)

Cairns on Great Shunner Fell.

Lovely Seat

Lovely Seat, 2,215 feet, is not a description of the fell's properties as a belvedere. In fact, it has nothing to to with either lovely or seat. Seat is, of course, the norse *saetr* or summer pasture, while lovely may be a corruption of *luin*, which was a Scandinavian word for an alarm or noise. Perhaps it was used to relay messages from the top of *sjonar fjall*, the lookout hill across the pass, to the settlers down in Thwaite. Locals call it Lunnerset. Possibly the men from the Ordnance Survey who drew up their maps over a century and a half ago misheard the name.

Lovely Seat stands towards the western end of a large area of high ground between Wensleydale and Swaledale which has the Buttertubs pass and the road over Oxnop Common as its western and eastern bounds. Both of these roads reach over 1,600 feet, thus making an ascent of the fell an easy prospect, particularly from the west where a walk of a mile following a wire fence, which whistles in the wind, leads to the summit. The eastern approach is much longer and is wet and boggy in places.

Most Pennine fells have a fair covering of peat which has accumulated over centuries. This brown-black layer is now subject to erosion and on Lovely Seat this degradation has led to the development of islands of peat standing up in areas of gritty sand and sparse grass. On one visit a camel-shaped remnant provided a much-welcomed seat for our two young children. As much as four feet of peat has been stripped from the fell top in places.

The summit cairn is large and squat and is composed of the local flags which have been quarried on the southern edge of the fell overlooking Hawes. A fine stone man to the west of the summit, slender and over six feet high, affords a good view of distant Ingleborough rising sphinx-like above the green valley of Widdale.

There is ample evidence on Lovely Seat of other past extractive industries dating from times when people thought little of any difference between countryside and town and when a man's span might be spent within a few miles of his birthplace and self-sufficiency was a necessity for all. Coal Gill drains south-east from the summit and there are several pits around the 1,500-foot contour, mirroring those on Great Shunner Fell across the Buttertubs road.

Sargill lead smelt mill is one of the best in the Pennines, its remoteness having ensured protection against the kind of treatment suffered by Blakethwaite on Rogan's Seat. The mill, which was only a fairly small concern, stands on the side of Sargill Beck and although the back wall and roof have gone, its former purpose is still recognisable. There is a waterwheel pit and a flue climbing 60 feet up the steep valley side to the stumpy remains of a square chimney. The mill was working for around 30 years until about 1870. About a quarter of a mile to the north-west is the level entrance where there are the remains of a dressing floor and spoil tips.

Lovely Seat's history may not do justice to its name, which anyway is gainsayed by the philologian, but to spend a few hours on the fell in the late spring with the curlews crying and the larks warbling is to experience a loveliness which suggests that the men from the Ordnance Survey had it right after all.

"The Big Country" as seen from south of Hawes. The distant peaks are Great Shunner Fell (left) and Lovely Seat (right). (Geoffrey N. Wright)

6
White Rose, Red Rose

The Wars of the Roses were dynastic rather than geographical, even though two of the most important battles – the second certainly being the bloodiest – Wakefield and Towton, were fought in Yorkshire. The wars, which finally threw up the Tudors and a period of peace which catapulted England from the medieval to the modern world, are remembered annually at Headingley and Old Trafford. The boundary between the White Rose and Red Rose counties follows a high Pennine ridge for but little of its course and only one summit, that of Green Hill, actually stands on the line. Gragareth's top is just in Lancashire but the more interesting parts of the fell are across the border and Great Coum has on its slopes the County Stone, an age-old marker of the meeting place of Yorkshire, Lancashire and Westmorland.

These three fells form a compact group which can be easily visited within a day's walk but which have enough of interest on and around them to encourage a more detailed look.

Gragareth

Gragareth, 2,057 feet, rises above the small and quiet village of Ireby and between the valleys of Leck Beck and Kingsdale Beck. The fell has a romantic, ancient-sounding name though the alternative Grey Garth is more descriptive. It has also been rendered as Gregareth and Gragreth.

There is an interesting description, in John Byng's *A Tour of the North* of 1792, of a journey between Weathercote and Yordas caves. The latter is on the east side of the hill. "Our guide was a merry, hearty fellow, and with much fun defended his County from our abuse, while we were crossing the terrible, stoney mountain called Gragareth – tho' he called it a short step and strided away, where from bog and stone, our horses could not keep pace with him, yet it appear's to me a distance of three miles. Crossing a nasty, stoney brook, we arrived at Yordas Cave."

This is a likely-sounding description but either Byng or, surely less likely, his guide was mistaken, for they must have been crossing West Fell on Whernside and the "stoney brook" was Kingsdale Beck.

Just as John Byng, one of the first Yorkshire Dales tourists, visited Yordas cave and spurned the fell above it, so today Gragareth is probably explored as much underground as over for many potholes and caves seam through the limestone base of the fell and on any given Bank Holiday there are almost certainly more people under the hill than on it.

The opportunities for subterranean exploration are numerous and range from the large chambers of Yordas Cave, which has been a tourist attraction for a couple of centuries and which can be explored by anyone with care, to the inconspicuous entrance to Lost John's on the other side of the fell which is a full-scale caving expedition for the experienced and properly equipped only. Lost John's gives access to the Leck Fell Master Cave, extending for nearly two miles and collecting the underground drainage from the whole of the fell. One of the great caving discoveries, it was first entered in 1928.

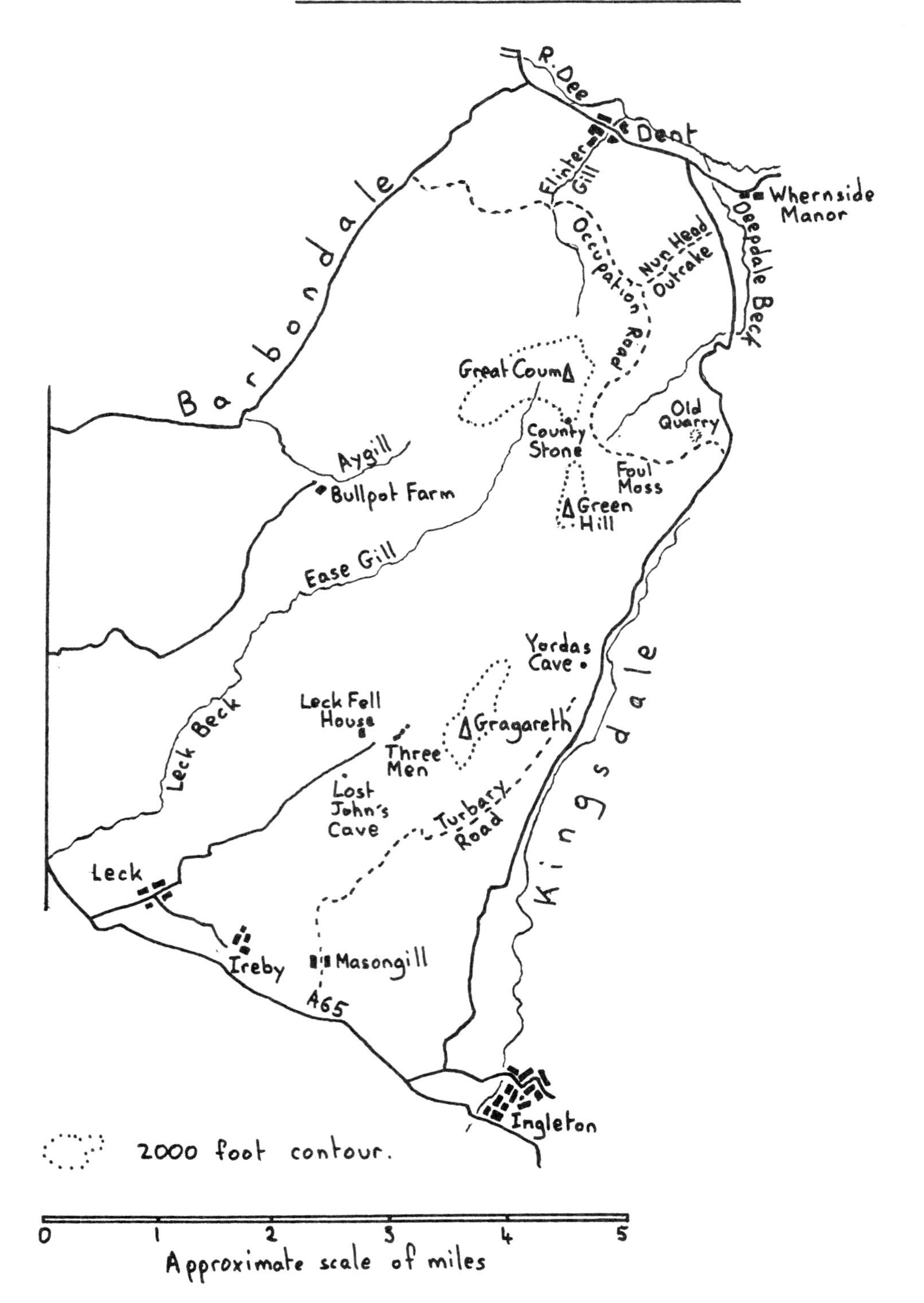
White Rose, Red Rose
R. Dee
Dent
Flinter Gill
Whernside Manor
Deepdale Beck
Occupation Road
Nun Head Outrake
Barbondale
Great Coum
Old Quarry
County Stone
Foul Moss
Aygill
Bullpot Farm
Green Hill
Ease Gill
Yordas Cave
Kingsdale
Leck Beck
Leck Fell House
Gragareth
Three Men
Lost John's Cave
Turbary Road
Leck
Ireby
Masongill
A65
Ingleton
2000 foot contour.
0 1 2 3 4 5
Approximate scale of miles

Gragareth's heart may be of limestone but its head is millstone grit, a fact illustrated by the coarseness of the vegetation and dampness of the ground high up as well as by the wall which runs the length of the summit ridge. The gritstone outcrops in places and fractures easily into slabs of a suitable size for building and the upper slopes are adorned with the results of a great deal of constructive effort.

The hill's pride are the Three Men of Gragareth which stand on the 1,650-foot contour above Leck Fell House, on the Lancashire side. These hoary cairns rise from a rash of gritstone near the end of the fell road from Leck. There are many pretenders nearby as well as a stone igloo which provides shelter for one in comfort or for two at a snug squeeze.

Leck Fell House, standing in quiet isolation at the end of the road, a thousand feet above and nearly three miles away from the hamlet of Leck, is one of the most remote of Pennine dwellings. The yard was full of sheep making noisy appeals for freedom on one cold, late October day but the lack of smoke from either chimney suggested that the house is no longer inhabited permanently. Perhaps it has reverted to its original role of *saeter*.

The tarmac ends here though the track continues for another couple of miles up the valley above Ease Gill to a shooting box, a long, low building, which provides five-star accommodation for sheep.

Gragareth's two enclosing valleys, that of Ease Gill and Leck Beck to the west, and Kingsdale to the east, show a marked contrast in form. Kingsdale bore the brunt of a glacier which crossed over from Dentdale and displays great expanses of bare rock and scars where the original soil cover was scraped away. The western valley was in the lee of the fells and escaped the glacial scouring which gives Kingsdale so much of its attractiveness. The fell was covered in ice, however, the creeping blanket of an ice sheet rather than the cutting edge of a glacier, and this has left a covering of boulder clay over the limestone, making the slopes dull and wet. The limestone, though unseen, is suspected for there are numerous swallow holes, funnel-shaped depressions marking the tops of pot holes.

The easiest ascent of Gragareth is from Leck Fell House whence a walk of three-quarters of a mile east-north-east leads to the summit, visiting the Three Men on the way. Apart from the latter, this is not a particularly inspiring journey and it has the disadvantage, to patriotic Yorkshire folk, of being entirely in Lancashire. Another ascent, following the county boundary wall from Over Hall near Ireby, is again only feasible on the Lancashire side for it uses a long and narrowing wedge of land which is walled on either side but has no cross-walls from its start to its finish just short of the top, while the Yorkshire side of the wall meets fourteen cross-walls in the same distance.

The best ascent for the county purist makes use of the Turbary Road, a grassy track formerly used for carting peat down from the fell. This can be gained by a right-of-way, crossing areas of limestone boulders and little escarpments, which climbs a ladder stile from a bend on the Kingsdale road a hundred or so yards south of the Twistleton Lane end. The Turbary Road is well worth following for its own sake as it leads through delightful limestone country passing close to a series of potholes well known to speleologists. Above Shout Scar the track climbs to meet a cross-wall on Bullpot Bank and here the hard work begins as the way is now upwards, beside the wall to a stile on the county boundary north of the summit. Alternatively, the Turbary Road can be deserted earlier and the fellside ascended over Dodson's Hill.

As stated, the summit is not in Yorkshire, though it is only a little the less for that, neither is it marked by the triangulation pillar (S5404) which stands just under 200 yards from the wall on a fairly featureless plateau broken by a few peat hags. No, the true top lies in between the two and will be recognised by the practised eye of the summiteer!

The view from the summit is dull in the near vicinity but improves with distance. Gragareth's western position means that the Lakeland fells are prominent across Morecambe Bay while in the other direction Whernside and Ingleborough dominate the scene.

The Pennine fells are scored with many miles of dry stone wall but there are few to match the one demarcating the county boundary on Gragareth. Its builders may have been aware of history, for it is certainly higher and more solidly built along the "Roses" stretch of the boundary than further north where it divides Yorkshire from Westmorland. This wall, like most on the hills, dates back to the eighteenth- and nineteenth-century enclosures of the high commons into fields of 30 acres or more.

The commissioners who decided on the allotment of the former commons drew their lines on the map with a ruler. The wallers followed, giving the geometrical patterns which we see today. Lower down, in the valleys, enclosures had been going on for centuries and the fields are smaller, less regular, and the walls more haphazard in their construction. In some areas building a wall was an efficient way of clearing stones and there may well be a correlation between field sizes and the original stoniness of the ground.

Most dry stone walls follow a regular pattern. They are based firmly on solid footings and really consist of two walls, tapering inwards towards the top and linked together by throughstones. These are vital in binding the structure together and were often left jutting out for it was laborious work to cut or find stones of the right length before they were built into the wall, and once there they could only be broken off at the cost of weakening the wall. Gaps in the middle of the wall were filled with small pieces or fillings and the wall was topped off with capstones. On the Gragareth boundary wall these lean against each other slantwise.

North of the summit, by a stile, the method of construction can be studied in detail for a cross-wall cuts through the main one and the wall end or *head* is in view. Next to it is a *cripple hole* or sheep creep which can be blocked with a large, flat slab. It goes without saying that the walker should avoid crossing a dry stone wall except by a stile or gate.

Walking north from the summit there is a thin patch, followed by the ubiquitous knobbly tyre tracks, which leads through an area of disturbed ground, source of the stone for the wall. The descent is very gradual indeed with only a hundred feet or so being lost in over a mile and when the slope starts to climb gently again, the walker is on the next of this trio of border fells.

Green Hill

Green Hill, 2,060 feet, occupies the middle position of the three summits on the broad ridge, well to the west of the main Pennine watershed, which runs from Ingleton to Dent. Its highest point is about halfway between those of its higher neighbours, Gragareth and Great Coum, and is marked by a cairn of a few stones on the Yorkshire side of the wall.

Green Hill will probably be crossed rather than climbed for its own sake, but should this course of action be chosen, then it is best to approach from the east: from Yorkshire, of course!

Dentdale, with Great Coum conspicuous in the distance. (John M. Capes)

The famous "Three Men of Gragareth".

Just on the Dentdale side of the road through Kingsdale a wide, walled track, the Occupation Road, heads off north-west and then south-west and then straight towards Green Hill. The track is not particularly dry underfoot but as it crosses first High Moss and then Foul Moss this is not entirely surprising. After Foul Moss the track, now unenclosed, swings round to the right and can be deserted for the fellside at the next gate to the left. A fairly steep pull up the hillside brings the visitor to the county wall.

One February, when the hills were gripped with ice, the ascent of Green Hill was an unexpected pleasure for the feet remained dry and we were able to sledge back down on a bivvy sack. An ascent from the west could be made be following the track, a continuation of the Leck Fell road, to where it ends just past the shooters' hut and then by striking up the fellside.

From the summit there is a generally gentle descent northwards to the col between Green Hill and Great Coum, named on the map as Saddle of Fells. A few shake holes here remind us that, although the summits of these hills are millstone grit, they are underlain with limestone.

Saddle of Fells is but three-quarters of a mile away from the last two-thousander along this ridge.

Great Coum

Great Coum, 2,250 feet, is the bulkiest as well as the highest of this threesome and, together with Whernside, it dominates the southern side of Dentdale, giving 161 feet in altitude to its better-known neighbour but nothing in sheer size.

Great Coum's northern slopes are girdled by a walled track, over 30 feet wide, running for 5½ miles between Deepdale Head and the Barbondale road. This, the Occupation Road as it is called locally, though named Green Lane on the maps, dates from the enclosure of the Dent common lands which occured as late as 1859. A study of the field boundaries on either side of the track shows that the earlier fields on the northern, downhill side are considerably narrower than the allotments above. Its route may well be that of an earlier track linking the numerous quarries and pits of the fellside and running above the original intake walls. Binks Quarry, below the steep slope east of the summit, was a source of the fossiliferous limestone which was polished up as Dent Marble.

Together with one of the steep and deep-cut tracks up from Dentdale, like Nun House Outrake or Flinter Gill, the Occupation Road makes an admirable approach to Great Coum. Flinter Gill especially, with its woods and waterfalls, is a delight.

Once on the Occupation Road there are choices of ways up to the summit. After a walk of a quarter of a mile west, another walled track, Wideron Gate, climbs to an opening on to a large hill pasture which has a sheepfold in its bottom corner and the summit wall at its top. It's a good mile between the two. Another ascent takes in the cairns and scree of the Megger Stones before following a wall over Crag End to the summit. The best route follows the Occupation Road eastwards for 2½ miles, with airy views of Dentdale and Deepdale, before turning off through a gate on the right, just past a ford over one of the tributaries of Gastack Beck whose fine waterfalls can be seen on the left. The walker has to make a decision about this, for a day which sees the waterfalls to their best effect, as tumbling white streaks against the green bowl-like head of the Gastack Beck valley, will also see this eastern end of the Occupation Road at its miry worst. This part, around the head of the valley and across Foul Moss, holds the worst stretches in contrast with the western end which is always a delight, living up to its name, as a green lane.

A pull up from the road leads to the ridge from Green Hill, near the County Stone. This massive erratic boulder stands five feet high and marks the former county boundary of the West Riding of Yorkshire, Lancashire and Westmorland. County Stone was an obvious and immovable choice of boundary mark for the dalesfolk who first divided this land, a sure stopping point on medieval beatings of the parish bounds of Dent, Casterton and Leck. Now it merely indicates a bend in the border between Lancashire and Cumbria. If bureaucrats visited such places and felt the history of them instead of just sitting in offices, drawing lines on maps, they might be less inclined to meddle.

This dumpy monolith is named prominently on John Speed's county maps of the early seventeenth century, correctly spelt on the West Riding version but appearing as "Coutie Stone" on the Lancashire map.

Not surprisingly, it has attracted the attention of chisellers and bears the inscriptions, weathered and lichened, of, among others, MC 1837 and WB 1900.

The old Lancashire-Yorkshire wall is heading due north and south where it abuts on both sides of the county stone and, although it is lower than on Gragareth, it is still made of fairly large gritstone blocks. In contrast, the Westmorland-Lancashire wall, heading off south-westwards to run beside Long Gill and Ease Gill, is composed of a thinner, slabby stone, as if recognising the inferior inter-county history of the latter two!

The present boundary between North Yorkshire and Cumbria follows another wall, dividing the parishes of Dent and Thornton in Lonsdale, which leaves the summit one just south of Green Hill's top.

The ascent of a third of a mile over Coal Pits Hill and past the large cairn on the scree rash of Gatty Pike brings the walker to the summit. The latest O.S. map shows this to be in the enclosure next to the one where the obvious cairn stands, but the walker approaching from Gatty Pike can easily search it out before crossing the wall. There's nothing to mark the spot anyway and the cairn is a more satisfactory place to halt. It is a tall, tapering, slender affair and it always tempts the visitor to balance just one more stone on its apex, a risky business which may one day topple the whole lot into the neighbouring depression, a good shelter, whence it originally came. It stands in an area of tussock grass with several small tarns nearby and commands good views, especially to the north-west where the Lakeland fells are prominent. In front of these is Green Combe with its vertical lines of dry stone walling. Further round are the Howgills, finely dappled on a day of sunshine and wind-driven clouds, and Baugh Fell rising above Aye Gill Pike. Behind Baugh Fell can be seen the almost vertical crag of Wild Boar Fell's gritstone summit. Dentdale is in view but Dent Town itself is hidden by the convexity of Great Coum's slopes. The dumpy top of Whernside contrasts with the magnificence of Ingleborough, two dales away to the south-south-east. Dentdale is well appreciated from the cairn on top of The Crag, a couple of hundred yards away to the north-west.

The walk may be continued round to the lower top of Crag Hill, 2,239 feet, although the latter looks higher from Great Coum. The illusion is not dispelled by visiting the Ordnance column on Crag Hill (S5661) to check, although a squint along the top of the trig point shows the surveyors to be correct. Anyone who has visited the other 2,000-foot Crag Hill, rising above Coledale in the Lake District, and is expecting similarities in anything other than name will be rather disappointed for the Yorkshire version has only a couple of islands of craggy ground in a sea of grass.

7
Round Garsdale and Grisedale

Swaledale, Wensleydale and Wharfedale: there are many who sing the praises of these fine Yorkshire valleys, but Garsdale, narrow and hemmed in, with no village to act as a focus and a rather industrial feel to its railwayed upper reaches, has fewer devotees. Its offshoot, Grisedale, is still less known, though it has revived a little since it featured on paper and screen a few years ago as "The Dale that Died". For the perceptive walker, however, both valleys and their surrounding fells hold much of interest.

Frederick Williams, author of that nineteenth-century study of enterprise *The Midland Railway*, obviously thought highly of Garsdale: "Here a different view from that with which we have become familiar appears; and instead of a wild and dreary waste, we have a kindlier clime and brighter scenes." He also hinted at the pre-railway inaccessibility of the area: "we may mention that every tip wagon here used by the contractor had to be brought by road up from Sedbergh, and that the carriage of them cost a guinea each."

The great bulk of Baugh Fell buttresses Garsdale to the north and, together with Swarth Fell Pike, hems in sequestered Grisedale. Southwards the narrow valley of the leaping River Clough gives way to the steep flanks of Rise Hill, with its summit Aye Gill Pike which is 175 feet short of a mention in this volume. The upper end of Garsdale is deflected north-eastwards by one of Williams's "vast hills".

Great Knoutberry Hill

Great Knoutberry Hill, 2,205 feet, certainly lives up to that description. It is the summit of a fifteen-square-mile wedge of highland between the upper reaches of Garsdale, Wensleydale, Dentdale and Widdale. The latter, a straight, short valley, marks the hill's south-eastern boundary and gives it its alternative name of Widdale Fell.

The hill lies on the Pennine watershed and the boundary between the north and west Ridings (now North Yorkshire and Cumbria) runs generally north to south across the fell.

Great Knoutberry Hill has had more miles of railway running across its flanks than any other Yorkshire 2,000-footer, it has a former station at the halfway mark (from sea-level, not from the valley!), is pierced by a tunnel, has several viaducts and cuttings, and any number of fine features of Victorian engineering. Its northern footings are the site of an epic struggle of man against mire, while a passenger could once catch a train from Dent Station to Garsdale and then walk back along a drove road which was for centuries part of another major route between Scotland and England.

The story goes that a visitor once enquired why Dent station was a good four miles from the township of the same name. "It'll be so it's near t'tracks" came the laconic local reply. For the walker who is interested in railways, there are few hills as worthy of attention as Great Knoutberry!

The way to the top, therefore, must start at Stone House Bridge, almost in the shadow of Artengill Viaduct. The beck has carved itself a deep, steep-sided valley and before the structure was started there was a 60-foot waterfall here.

The viaduct is over 200 yards long and has eleven arches, each with a 45-foot span. Two of the piers, one on either side of the gill, are of extra thickness and

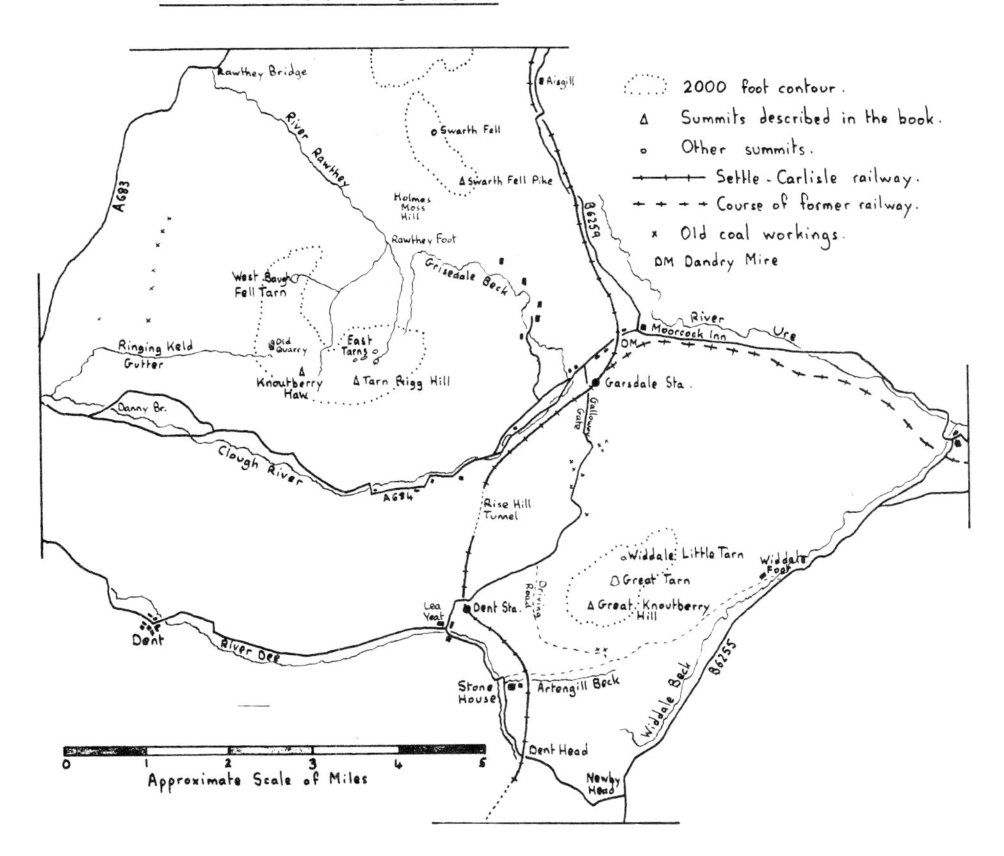

one of the stones, a giant even by Settle-Carlisle standards, measures fourteen by six feet and is a foot thick, weighing more than eight tons. The piers are made from the local 'Dent marble' while the arches are of gritstone from Kelbeck, to the east of the line. Here a large culvert takes the beck under the line down a series of steps. At its maximum height, the viaduct is 117 feet above the beck. As with many of the works on this most confident of Victorian undertakings, problems were met and in order to stand the foundations of the piers on solid rock, they had to be sunk as deep as 55 feet.

A four-car diesel multiple unit which crossed during one visit looked like a toy train as it busily made its way north. This line was built to carry grander stuff.

The Dent 'marble' which makes up much of the structure is a fossiliferous limestone quarried below Dent Head Viaduct and at several other sites around Garsdale and Dent. The rock was cut and polished at the mills of Stone House Marble Works which worked from the early nineteenth until the beginning of this century. It was a major local employer in mid-Victorian times when marble, whether geologically genuine or not, was a fashionable stone. As well as using the local 'black marble' and another grey crinoidal limestone, the mills also imported Italian marbles and made a wide range of goods from inkstands to tombstones. The mills, one of which had a 60-foot diameter water wheel, were demolished in 1928.

They had a part to play in the establishment of one of north-east England's major engineering works, for in 1835 a 25-year-old William George Armstrong came on a fishing holiday to Dentdale. He was so fascinated by the intricate system of water power at the mills that he gave up the idea of becoming a solicitor and dedicated himself to hydraulic engineering. Thus Armstrong's of Tyneside began.

The track up Arten Gill is an old pack-horse route from Dentdale over the shoulder of the fell to Widdale Bridge and it can be followed for a mile or so until a wall following the county boundary is met at a gate where the track becomes totally unenclosed.

From here an easy ascent follows the wall to the summit, where two fences and a line of posts meet the wall. The top is graced by a short and dumpy trig point (S8285) and a wall shelter. I found a baby's dummy in the shelter on one visit, the "calm of hills above" having obviously rendered its use unnecessary.

The views are best towards the west but if desolation is sought then the new fence will be followed towards the north-east and Widdale Fell. I was standing by this fence, built on the remains of a tumbled wall and 50 yards from the shelter, wondering whether to carry on through the mist and rain to the lower top when I was approached by that particular hilltop menace, the unsolicited advice giver. He was halfway through a long, and wrong, lecture on map reading before I interrupted him, politely, to point out that not everyone who stands and stares is necessarily lost. And I'd come up here for a bit of peace!

The top of Widdale Fell, with its twin tarns, Great and Little, is a mess of peat hags and groughs and, although not in the same league as Lune Forest under Mickle Fell, it certainly impedes progress. When the marble mills at Stone House were in full production, Widdale Great Tarn was harnessed as a water supply and in times of drought an old man was employed to climb the fell in the morning to set the water on and at night to turn it off. A long and lonely ridge descends north-eastwards over Little Knoutberry Hill and Sandy Hill.

A line of fence posts leads down from the summit of Great Knoutberry Hill to the minor road between Dentdale and Garsdale, where a track leaves the road to contour round under the western and southern slopes. The 'Driving Road' is part of one of the former Scottish drove routes and is known, in its tarred section further north, as 'Galloway Gate'. On Great Knoutberry it follows a grassy ledge below the cairns on Pikes Edge and above small limestone scars for part of the way and gives fine views of Dentdale and Whernside. Crinoids can be found along some stretches, the fossil stems of sea creatures which form the grey limestone polished up to such good effect in the valley below, and this level, dry track contrasts strongly with the one beside Arten Gill. Near the head of Arten Gill are the remains of coal workings, again reminding us of the industrial activity which was once so much a part of what we now see as The Countryside.

Where Great Knoutberry slims to the col between itself and Rise Hill, a pass long followed by a track from Dentdale to Garsdale, the Midland engineers drove Risehill Tunnel. The visitor standing on this recently tree-covered depression can only wonder at the stamina of men who lived in the temporary village built here which had huts, sheds and storerooms at a height of 1,300 feet. They spent their days 140 feet below, drilling holes in solid rock with hammers and jumpers and illuminated by candlelight. Ironically the rock turned out to be less solid than anticipated and the tunnel had to be lined for three-quarters of its length with masonry. Three hundred and fifty people lived up here and a tramway ran down to Garsdale. No doubt the navvies walked down to Lea Yeat in Dentdale where a brewery had a short-lived heyday during construction.

On the very northern slopes of Great Knoutberry, at Garsdale Head, is Dandry Mire Viaduct and the remains of Hawes Junction. The viaduct was not scheduled on the Midland Railway's original plans: an embankment was to be constructed, but after two years of tipping more than a quarter of a million cubic yards of spoil it was realised that an alternative would have to be sought. The muck went in all right but all it did was push the peat out of the way, forming a bank on each side up to fifteen feet high in places. Dandry Mire – the very name is enough to break hearts. In the end a viaduct of twelve arches was built, 50 feet high, with a further fifteen to get down to anything solid enough to put foundations on.

A branch line to Hawes following the head of Wensleydale was opened from Hawes Junction in 1878. Here stood Garsdale Station with its signal-box, water tank and turntable. On one particularly stormy night a locomotive was being turned when things got out of control. The engine only stopped revolving hours later when someone had the bright idea of tipping ashes into the turntable pit to clog up the works. Shortly afterwards a fence of sleepers was built to prevent any further carouselling.

At the time of writing the threat which has hung over the future of the Settle-Carlisle line for several years seems to have lifted. Politicians in London who can see no further than next year's balance sheet viewed the line as a liability within the scheme of 'modern enterprise' but after a battle lasting from August 1983 to April 1989, the tables were turned and the line saved. During that time, thanks to public interest brought about largely as a result of a vigorous campaign by the Settle-Carlisle Joint Action Committee, the number of passengers increased from under 100,000 to half a million. Money will have to be spent in order to affirm the rightful place in history of this truly mighty undertaking and the Settle and Carlisle Railway Trust has been founded to play a vital part in this. This is a registered charity which plans to raise four and a half million pounds to restore stations and other buildings that are now surplus to British Rail's requirements for operating the line. The trust will also contribute towards the preservation of the great engineering works such as Ribblehead Viaduct below Whernside, the deterioration through neglect of which was one of the main excuses put forward for the closure of the line.

The Settle-Carlisle has been through traumas before and lived to tell the tale. Back in 1966 Bill Mitchell and David Joy were questioning whether the line would see its centenary. It achieved this milestone a decade later accompanied with much celebration. The Midland, its engineers and its host of navvies, built things to last.

Looking west from the former Garsdale station or north-west from Great Knoutberry's summit, a vast, rotund fell rising to a dumpy top, or rather two tops, hems in Garsdale on its north side.

Baugh Fell

Baugh Fell has two summits, Knoutberry Haw and Tarn Rigg Hill, half a mile apart across a peaty plateau. These tops give a good demonstration of how things cartographic can change for on the old Ordnance Survey maps the former was given a height of 2,216 feet while the latter was shown as being somewhere over 2,200 feet. Knoutberry Haw's predominance was recognised by the ultimate OS accolade, a trig point. The latest map, dated 1985 and compiled from large-scale sheets surveyed between 1969 and 1979, shows the situation reversed with Tarn Rigg Hill being elevated to 2,224 feet, a full seven feet higher than the latest figure for Knoutberry Haw which has risen one foot as a consolation prize! All this will seem academic after the climb to the top, anyway.

Baugh, is generally pronounced as in Brummell or Diddley, but the local pronunciation is Barfel. Its steep southern slopes rush down to Garsdale accompanied by a cascade of walls, thus precluding ascents from the valley. Approaches can be made from several other directions, though these will be long, mostly pathless, wet and solitary.

A welter of tracks ascends the lower western slopes but all fade out around the 1,000-foot mark. A glance at the Ordnance map will show why, for there is a line of disused pits in the base of the gritstone which forms Baugh Fell's immense cap. Here it is about 500 feet thick though nowhere does it form crags as on neighbouring Swarth and Wild Boar fells. The tracks can at least be used to cross the enclosed intake land of the lower slopes, after which an ascent can be made over a long mile or so of wet moor to the plateau in the vicinity of West Baugh Fell Tarn.

Several cairns stand along the plateau edge and are visible from below. The tarn itself, a large sheet of water but one which disconcertingly disappears in its flat surroundings, stands at about 2,050 feet and drains away eastwards into Rawthey Gill.

The latter can be used as a fine route of ascent, providing the most scenically interesting ways up the fell from Rawthey Bridge on the A683. The Rawthey is a true river down by the bridge. It can be followed to its source above Gill Head through scenery which starts in the sylvan surroundings of Uldale, continues in the miniature gorge of Dockholmes and, after a right-angled turn, climbs up a ravine and past a sheepfold before opening out on to the broad top below the trig point on Knoutberry Haw. As an alternative, a diversion up Tarn Gill and then south along the plateau will arrive at the same point.

The easiest way of reaching the trig point is to follow the wall up from Garsdale Foot. A minor road descends from the A684 to cross the Clough River at Danny Pridge, where deep, shady pools will tempt you to linger on a hot day, before climbing to meet the road to Garsdale Foot and High Fawes. A gate leads to an untidy track climbing alongside a beck by a wire fence. Soon the fence turns to point towards the fell and is replaced by a wall, much more natural in these surroundings. At first it looks as if the top section of the wall is very steep but closer inspection reveals this to be another one, coming up from Garsdale.

The wall is accompanied, first on one side then on the other, by Ringing Keld Gutter. On one very hot ascent, in a dry spell of weather during one of the finest English summers in memory, there was not enough water to make the gutter ring and barely enough to cover the feet. They were sorely in need of cooling, having walked round all the Howgill Fells 2,000-foot tops already during the day, but what water there was trickling down the stones was lukewarm!

Towards the top of the climb, where the slope steepens, a zigzag groove eases the climb. There is a disused stone quarry on the plateau above and no doubt the stone was carted or brought down by sled here.

Once above this the wall turns more to the south-east and climbs gently to the trig point on Knoutberry Haw. This carries OS Benchmark S5662 and stands at a wall junction. Half a mile to the east, across some wet ground with a peaty tarn in the middle, lies the true summit, Tarn Rigg Hill. The wall between the two tops bends to the south as a mark of respect to the intervening mire and in normal conditions it is best to stay close to it.

Tarn Rigg Hill is well named for it has more standing water on it than any other Yorkshire fell top, a cluster of half a dozen bright tarns, shining in contrast to their stony and peaty surroundings, lying to the north of the summit. Sand from the Baugh Fell tarns was once prized for its sharpening qualities. Mixed with grease, it was scraped into a board with holes in it and this *strickle* was kept with the scythe.

According to the map, the summit is just over the wall, at a kink by a junction, but that need not bother us for the top is so flat that this side of the wall will do. It will certainly suit the farmer better. There is no cairn.

Anyone who has got thus far will want to sit down and admire the view which, from such a flat top, is surprisingly extensive. Near at hand is the full breadth of Baugh Fell itself, sprinkled with tarns and rashes of boulders, peaty expanses and swathes of dull green. Several cairns stand on the plateau rim, shepherds' marks sometimes built in pairs, with a particularly fine one visible in line with Hugh Seat on Mallerstang Edge.

Further away Wild Boar Fell and Swarth Fell are prominent across the Rawthey and Grisedale with the Mallerstang tops around to the north-east. Looking back along the wall, the Lakeland fells show their rugged skyline with the Scafell Pike to Great End ridge visible just above the trig point. Through the wide gap between the Howgills and Wild Boar Fell, the upper Eden Valley is backed by the high Pennines, from Cross Fell to Mickle Fell. Looking south, across the wall, the Three Peaks can be seen, though Ingleborough is almost hidden by Whernside. Great Knoutberry Hill and Great Coum also show up well in this direction.

Grisedale, valley of the wild pigs, once tamed and now reverting to wilderness, can be used as a starting point for a walk up to Tarn Rigg Hill. A path follows the valley from Moor Rigg, up past the former farms of East Scale and Round Ing, sad places these, on to the open moor. Although an ascent could be made from here, the best route follows the tongue of land between Grisedale Gill and Haskhaw Gill, although the farmer at East House does not look kindly on anyone straying from the right of way through to Uldale. This is a fine enough walk in itself, especially when the cloud is down on the tops.

All water draining off Baugh Fell, and with over 80 inches of rain a year there is plenty of it, finds its way into the River Clough or the Rawthey and eventually into the Lune. The strip of moor between Grisedale and Haskhaw gills is the Baugh Fell watershed, for Haskhaw Gill and all streams westwards join the Rawthey while Grisedale Gill and becks to the east feed the Clough.

The walker who uses the route to Grisedale on the descent will very quickly become aware that the hill rising across the top of the Rawthey-Grisedale valley is becoming larger by the minute. No matter, this is our next top and it is one which has a little more of the mountain flavour about it than Baugh Fell.

Swarth Fell Pike

Swarth Fell Pike, 2,125 feet, stands on the boundary between the West Riding and Westmorland, while the North Riding is very close. The boundary between the two ridings follows the ridge from Garsdale Head almost to the summit and the county line carries on along the ridge over the higher (2,235 feet) Swarth Fell before following Needlehouse Gill down to the Rawthey valley. Unusually, the summit of the higher fell is not on the boundary but stands fifty yards within Westmorland. The reason for this seeming anomaly is the practical one that the boundary follows a wall and not the very highest ground. Only the chauvinist would climb the pike without going on to the fell and it would not be thought too remiss if the walker carried on for a further mile within Westmorland to visit the magnificent Wild Boar Fell.

Swarth Fell Pike is the peak or pointed end of the black hill, for Swarth is derived from the old Norse *svartr* which is a close relation of swarthy. The blackest bit of Swarth Fell Pike is half a mile south-west of the summit where the ovoid Holmes Moss Hill swells above the head of the Rawthey valley. A fence, much mended with an assortment of ironmongery and wood, crosses this excruciatingly wet top, as good a place as any to imagine Bunyan's Pilgrim in his slough.

As might be expected of a place with so much liquid underfoot, the Pennine watershed is close at hand, being followed by the former West Riding and North Riding boundary. Streams draining from Swarth Fell Pike end up in three major river systems, the Ure, Eden and Lune. This may not always have been the case, for the alignment of Grisedale suggests that its beck formerly joined the head of the Ure and that it may have been diverted by the same glacial deposits which caused the Midland Railway's engineers so many problems around Garsdale Head. Another school of thought argues that Grisedale Beck had already been captured by the River Clough in pre-glacial times. During the ice ages, Grisedale would have held a lake whose waters carved out the gorge now visible near Clough House. All in all, this is a fascinating area for the student of rivers, for Swarth Fell Pike looks down on another piece of riverine banditry, the capture of the Ure's headwaters by the Eden.

Rivers cut their valleys downwards but also slowly eat their way upstream. As a result, two neighbouring river systems will eventually confront each other where their headwaters meet. The more powerful stream, that which has cut the deeper valley, will thus syphon off some water from its rival and divert it into its own channel. The Eden and the Clough are both eating their way back inexorably towards the stretch of the Ure between Ure Crook and the Moorcock Inn and it is only a matter of time, though admittedly geological time, before that part of the river flows westwards.

Perhaps this fluvial confusion results in the fact that, although the land south of Swarth Fell Pike's summit is now said to be in the South Lakeland district of Cumbria, it is in the Yorkshire North constituency for European bureaucratic purposes!

A footpath between Grisedale and Lunds crosses the lower reaches of the ridge up to Swarth Fell Pike at a neat col by Turner Hill. It is a simple matter to follow the ridge up to the summit with backward glances to a lengthening Wensleydale as a reward for the small effort involved. Most of the hill is unenclosed so any number of other approaches can be devised. Smithy Gill leads almost directly from the road near Aisgill to the top while the peat lover will want to try the trudge over Holmes Moss Hill. Part of Aisgill Moor is named Foulmart Hill, a reference to the polecat.

The summit is crossed by a fence and is marked by a cairn of stones. Nearby is a small tarn. This is a good spot from which to study the scars on Wild Boar Fell but, apart from the cairn itself, there is a lack of dry seating and anyway, the view is much better from Swarth Fell!

Looking westwards a group of dumpy green hills appears, most unlike anything else in high Yorkshire, tempting the walker to abandon the main Pennine fells for their green and rounded tops.

A round of Swarth Fell

THE day was Whitsuntide Tuesday of 1941, and when we first looked up the valley from the Moorcock, the weather was an enigma. The barometer had remained at "fair" over-night, the clouds seemed fairly high, though rather thick but showed no sign of clearing off under the influence of the sun. However, as optimists in holiday mood, we thought "Nothing venture — nothing won" as we walked along the road to Shaw Paddock. Passing under the railway arch there, we struck directly up the fell, past a deserted farmstead and up the side of a gill on what is supposed to be a track to High Flust in Grisedale. Little sign of a track did we see, but, carefully choosing our way between two nasty-looking peat hags we reached the main ridge and turned right along it for Swarth Fell. How we appreciated the funny little sheep-trods here-abouts!

Just below the first of the "stone men" on Swarth Fell, we hit the cloud ceiling, and began to feel a dreary clamminess as well as the somewhat biting east wind we had become more and more aware of as we had made height. Also, our range of vision was now little more than nil, but we reached the second cairn without much difficulty.

Here it was that our plans went astray. We "carried on" keeping near the centre of the ridge so far as we knew, presently reaching an edge. So little did we suspect what had happened that, forgetting that we had not actually observed the third cairn on Swarth Fell, we descended from the edge, expecting to see at any moment the little tarn on the saddle between Swarth Fell and Wild Boar Fell. Alas! it did not appear, and when we dropped below cloud level again the prospect before us was unexpected.

The outing had been a disappointment: yet there had been compensations in that at least we had crossed Swarth Fell; and East Baugh Fell in conditions which; had we been aware of them, might have kept us off the "tops" altogether. And, we had enjoyed, under the best of conditions, the really delightful scenery of Upper Garsdale.

Yes, there was a deep and winding cleft in the fell side across the valley, which could be no other than Rawthay Gill on Baugh Fell. So — what?

We had little inclination to try to correct our mistake by making height again, especially as conditions overhead showed no real sign of improvement, so we regretfully admitted to ourselves that Wild Boar Fell (which we had not even seen on that day) was safe from our intrusion. Instead, we made a descending traverse to our left, in due time reaching a sheepfold in a gully, down which we quickly dropped to the valley bottom, finding ourselves first at Round Ing and then at Scale, both of them isolated farms at the head of Grisedale.

A.H. Robertshaw
(The Yorkshire Dalesman, April 1942)

8
The Howgill Fells

The Yorkshire fell walker serves a full apprenticeship of bog hopping and grough crossing, of steering tortuous courses over wet plateau tops or through ankle-deep heather and of devising routes along, or which try to avoid, a complexity of walls. The Howgill Fells have none of these normal attractions but possess a singularity which sets them apart and which welcomes the walker again and again back to their gentleness. "A change is as good as a rest" might well be the cry of the walker who has spent a few wet days in the environs of Yockenthwaite Moor, Great Knoutberry Hill or Darnbrook Fell, good as they are, and the Howgills provide that essential contrast.

Local farming practice favours an open-range approach and so, once clear of the valley pastures and intakes, usually below the 1,000-foot mark, the land is unenclosed. The exception to prove the rule is the fenced-in upper reach of Hobdale Gill, below the summit of Calders.

Named after a small hamlet halfway down the western side of the range, the fells are shaped rather like a hand, with fingers stretching out to the north from knuckles in the vicinity of the highest point, The Calf, and with the wrist slimming down over the lesser hill of Winder.

The old Yorkshire and Westmorland border, perpetuated by the Yorkshire Dales National Park boundary, runs across the highest land in the Howgills and several summits raise their heads above 2,000 feet. Four of these are judged worthy of separate mention here.

The Calf

The Calf, 2,218 feet, is the only Yorkshire 2,000-foot hill to be graced with the definite article, presumably in respect of its local importance. It is the highest and most central of the Howgill Fells and its summit can be reached from many directions and by way of a fine variety of walks.

The royal road to The Calf runs up from Sedbergh. The broad track is tramped by many as it follows the Howgills watershed, for although all rain falling on the fells eventually ends up in the Lancashire Lune, that which flows down the eastern slopes does so only after joining the Rawthey.

For an ascent which combines the highest top with the Howgill's most exciting feature, the walk will begin at the Cross Keys, a temperance hotel on the A683 Sedbergh-Kirkby Stephen road. The Howgills are convex hills so the initial approaches tend to be steep and this is certainly the case here, once the river pastures are crossed. They also generally present a picture of green slopes broken by occasional rashes of stones. These features and much more, including their fauna and flora – I once walked on the Howgills and Baugh Fell during the same, hot day and was plagued with flies only on the latter – is a result of the underlying rocks. In contrast to the rest of the Yorkshire 2,000-foot fells which are composed of carboniferous rocks, the Howgills are made of older stuff of the Silurian era.

This hard grey sandstone, mostly Coniston Grit, is further toughened at Cautley by tuffs and lavas which have formed Cautley Crags and the Spout. The

The lovely outlines of the superb Howgills, seen in low evening light. (Tom Parker)

Cautley Crags and Spout, one of the best-known features of the Howgills. (Brian Bradley)

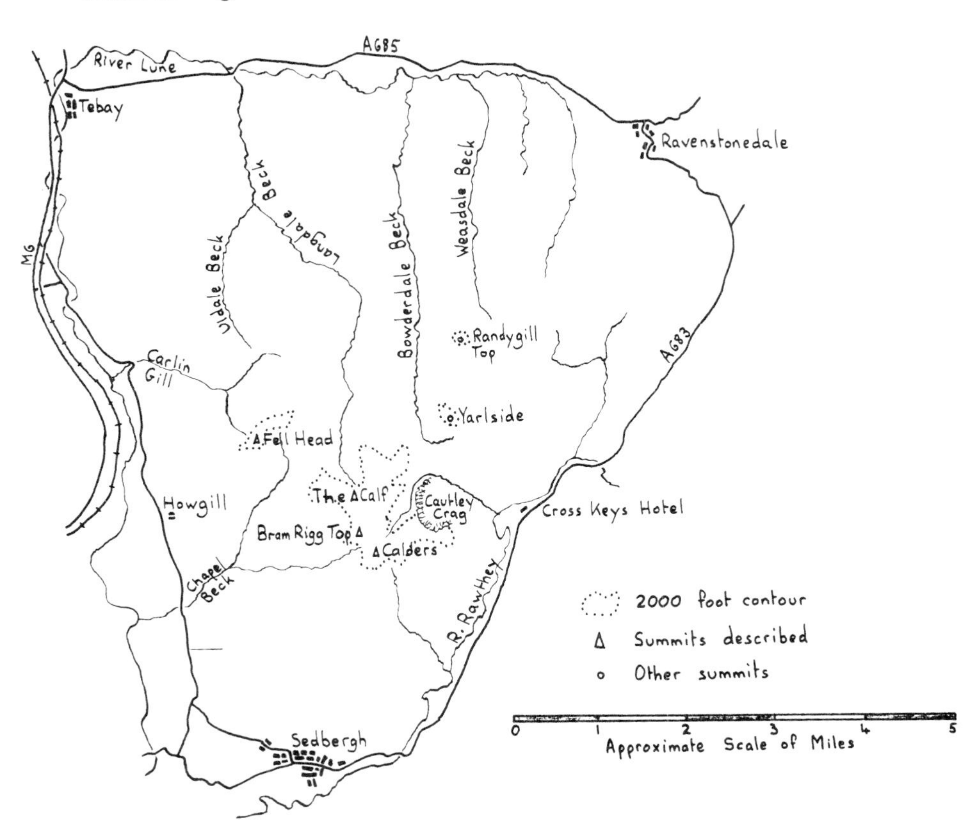

crags are impressive though not attractive to rock climbers, being too broken up with ledges and vegetation. Through a series of waterfalls, Cautley Holme Beck loses about 500 feet in a fifth of a mile. The upper falls cascade down through a series of steps and rapids but the main Spout is a real waterfall, a white mare's tail against the black rock, visible from the road a mile away. There are rowans and ferns in abundance in the gorge which is a shady paradise on a hot day and a ringside seat after a spell of wet weather.

Two ways climb beside the falls, a steep struggle up the north bank, or a more gentle green track which is heading for Bowderdale Head. This well-graded path is known as Scots' Rake, for local tradition tells of part of Bonnie Prince Charlie's army retreating this way in 1745. At Bowderdale Head a ruined, stone sheepfold stands near its modern-day counterpart of wire and corrugated sheets. The one blends in with the landscape and even in its ruined state has more of a look of permanence than the other.

Bowderdale, a long, steep-sided valley, is typical of the dales which have been etched into the northern Howgills. A bridleway follows the valley up from Bowderdale Foot and can be used as a steady route for ascending The Calf. It deserts the beck below the head of the valley by which time the pedestrian will have already covered nearly five miles and will probably have met nothing but the local black-faced Rough Fell sheep.

Distant Ingleborough. From Kidhow Gate.

Birks Fell Tarn.

The Howgill Fells.

Cairns on Great Shunner Fell.

Young Ure on Sails.

Punchard Coal Level, Water Crag.

Artengill Viaduct.

Swarth Fell Pike from Holmes Moss.

Mallerstang Edge.

Occupation Road, Great Coum.

Kidhow Gate.

The County Stone.

Yockenthwaite.

Peat erosion, summit of Darnbrook Fell.

Mickle Fell's summit.

Penyghent from above Penyghent Gill.

The Howgill Fells

ROUGH Fell sheep graze on the Howgill Fells. Even on The Calf, at 2,220 feet above sea-level and the highest of the Howgills, they are unperturbed by the wind which rips up the valleys to the west.

The Rough Fells are unprotected by walls or fences. There are unlimited grazing rights on the open fells: fells which are dissected by deep ravines and lively water-courses. Sheep tracks vanish overnight in foul weather, becoming part of the scree which litters their slopes. Stream beds are a jumble of boulders of all shapes and sizes.

The Rough Fells are as much a part of the Howgills as farmers in a score or so farms in the valleys below. These farms rarely change hands; when they do, new folk seldom stay here for long.

High Hill Farm, whose land and sheep are rented by Thomas Hood, is now derelict. It is passed by walkers making for The Calf from Sedbergh. You cannot see The Calf from the town. It shows itself at Calders, less than a half-mile from the summit.

This summit is disappointing. It is an almost insignificant mound among a range of high, rounded fells. You might look for a higher peak but there is none. An ugly, concrete Ordnance Survey pillar affords little shelter from the west wind which nearly always prevails during an ascent. No sooner has the visitor reached the summit than he wants to leave. The panorama of the Lakeland hills, Whernside, Ingleborough and Penyghent, the fells to the east and the coastlands to the west, can be studied at an equal advantage during the ascent.

Yorkshire nods at Westmorland between the smaller summits of The Calf plateau. The Yorkshire Dales National Park (West Riding Section) boundary runs along the county border close to the summit. The Calf, Crook, Winder, Arrant Haw, Brant Fell and Cautley Crags are all part of Yorkshire's share of the Howgills.

Baugh Fell, across the Cautley valley, is only four feet lower than The Calf. Its tarns were once frequented by farmers for their sand, said to contain some form of salt. Farmers would dip a piece of wood in pitch and while the pitch was still hot, coat it with the sand. The sticks provided ideal instruments on which to sharpen scythes.

The Howgills are Yorkshire's only slate mountains. The old Silurian rocks are exposed in grand style at Cautley Crags where they rise 2,000 feet above the valley bottom. Here too, Red Gill Beck descends over 600 feet in a series of cascades to form Cautley Spout. It is reached easily from The Calf and this route provides an exhilarating round trip from Sedbergh.

Ian Plant
(The Dalesman, March 1969)

For those who have climbed up from Cautley, the ascent from Bowderdale Head up to the bridleway is a simple one and the views down the long valley to the high Pennines are very rewarding.

The bridleway climbs up on to the plateau and bifurcates just before a small, anonymous tarn. It does not visit the top but one section skirts round to the north before descending White Fell to Castley, while the other leg heads south-west to drop down Bram Rigg to Birkhaw. On the ground a plain path does make for the summit which is graced by an Ordnance Survey trig point, benchmark S5676.

It is the only Howgill two-thousander to possess a trig point though two more appear on lesser local heights, Middleton Fell (1,593 feet) to the north and Winder (1,551 feet) above Sedbergh to the south. There is generally a small collection of begging sheep around the trig point nowadays. They still seem content to wait for gifts to be offered and are not nearly as streetwise as their sisters on Ingleborough.

The view is good and extensive. Collectors of county tops (those of the real counties, of course) should have a field day. Scafell Pike in Cumberland, Westmorland's Helvellyn, Lancashire's Old Man of Coniston and the Yorkshire pair, Mickle Fell in the North Riding and Whernside in the West Riding, are all in view. Also prominent are Cross Fell and, for the wrong reasons, Great Dun Fell, as well as a dozen or so Yorkshire 2,000-foot tops. All Three Peaks are in sight though Ingleborough, for once, is the least visible, being mostly hidden by Calders.

Closer at hand the Howgills roll and swell, a sea of heaving green flecked by a pale spray of white bent, a grass which, covering large areas, gives a bleached look to the tops. The other Yorkshire 2,000-foot tops are in view as is Randygill Top (2,051 feet), in Westmorland. Yarlside (2,096 feet), which also lies north of the county boundary, is hidden from view by The Calf's broad north-eastern ridge, itself an easy way up to the summit over West Fell and Hazelgill Knott.

Another wide ridge, this one heading to the north-west, leaves The Calf's summit and can be followed for an undulating 1½ miles to Yorkshire's most westerly 2,000-foot top.

Fell Head

Fell Head, 2,100 feet, has yet to be accurately surveyed, the height given here being an estimate based on the latest Ordnance Survey contours. The old one inch map put the height at somewhere above 2,050 feet but did not show a 2,100-foot contour nor did it give a spot height for the summit, only for the lower, 2,045-foot, western top. The most recent survey shows the summit in a contour ring equivalent to 2,099 feet and as the top rises but little in the vicinity of the cairn, 2,100 seems like a fair estimate.

Anyway, a few feet are nothing when put beside the enjoyment of getting to the top and the view from it.

Fell Head is well named, rising above the deeply incised Long Rigg Beck which lies to its southern side and the Ulgill becks, Great and Little, which gather on its northern slopes. It falls away steeply to the Lune Valley on the west and its only gentle slopes are those which join it with the main Howgills ridge at Breaks Head.

The easiest approach to Fell Head is from The Calf and this route, over White Fell Head and Bush Howe, is straightforward and gives good views. Indeed, on a really clear day, the Nine Standards which look down on Kirkby Stephen can be seen, above Randygill Top, from the vicinity of Breaks Head.

More exciting ways up can be made from the west as various paths leave the Fairmile Road, part of an old Roman route between Ribchester and Low Borrow Bridge. The Lune Valley narrows here, between the Howgills and Greyrigg Common, and travellers have been channelled through this gap for millenia. Roman road, turnpike road (now the A685), railway and the M6 motorway squeeze into a quarter-mile gap just north of here. The handicap of climbing from such a historic routeway is the incessant noise from the motorway, a background din that reaches to the summit on a calm day. From Beck Houses, a footpath climbs the lower slopes of Brown Moor before contouring round to the north. Above Whins End it can be left and the steep slopes of Fell Head tackled. Traffic noises are soon displaced by panting and drumming in the ears. A less vigorous climb can be had by following the path for a further half-mile and going up from the col between Fell Head and its western buttress, Linghaw.

The best way to the top of Fell Head follows Carlin Gill from the bridge on Fairmile Road. The walking is straightforward and easy at first, but after crossing Small Gill it becomes exciting with scrambling along the stream bed or sides in the vicinity of Black Force. A visit to the Spout, a 30-foot waterfall, should be made while in Carlin Gill. It is possible to scramble up on the left side of the Spout to reach gentler ground above. A sharp pull gains the ridge which can be followed by Over Sale and Breaks Head to the summit of Fell Head. Alternatively the left side of Black Force can be climbed and Little Ulgill Beck followed to just below the top. The area round Black Force and the Spout is the most interesting in the Howgills and ought to be visited for its own sake, even if Fell Head is not the ultimate aim of the day.

Whichever route is followed to the summit, the visitor will want to sit and enjoy the view from the fine cairn with its protruding pole. Here swifts were skimming the fellside, trawling the air for insects on a July day while, 200 feet lower, half a dozen dark brown fell ponies were patiently grazing through the heat of the day. On another occasion we disturbed a skylark which crouched and moved as if it were injured, drawing us away from its nest.

As Fell Head juts out to the west more than the other Howgill tops, it is a good vantage point for studying the Lakeland skyline. The great gash of Mickledore between Scafell and the Pike looks angular, rather as if it has been chopped out of the mountains. I have watched it from here with a tongue of white cloud pouring through. It was easy to imagine the glacier which had gouged it out, rising from Wasdale and slowly descending into upper Eskdale. I didn't know whether to feel pity or envy for the folk on Great Gable which was regularly covered and then uncovered by cloud: they might only be getting an intermittent view but at least it would be cooler there. It was certainly less busy on Fell Head. In four hours I had met no one but I could see the paths up the Old Man and Bowfell. The summit is a good place from which to watch the motorway climbing to Shap with its vast quarry. Further to the north lies Penrith. The dull drone of traffic is sometimes obscured by the louder hiss of a train. Sometime I shall come and sit up here at night and watch the light show.

The Howgill Fells are compact enough to make a visit to all the 2,000-foot tops (even those in Westmorland!), a distinct possibility for a day's walk. A suggested itinery, starting and ending at Cautley, is Randygill Top, Yarlside, Fell Head, The Calf, Bram Rigg Top and Calders. An hour per summit is a good average but the more time spent on the fells, the greater the reward. The fell on which least time will probably be spent is the next in this series.

River Rawthey below Rawthey Bridge, with Great Dummacks and the Howgills ahead.
(Geoffrey N. Wright)

Bram Rigg Top

Bram Rigg Top, 2,205 feet, the brambly or broomy ridge, is a very subsidiary top between The Calf and Calders. It is only a third of a mile south of The Calf and the drop between the two is not much more than a very gentle hundred feet. The path between Sedbergh and The Calf does not visit the summit but passes a couple of hundred yards to the east. It is interesting to compare the path south of The Calf, wide and worn, with its extension northwards over Bush Howe to Fell Head. It is obvious that: 1. most visitors approach from Sedbergh and 2. most only get as far as The Calf.

A bridleway leaves the Lune Valley at Birkhaw to curve round under the top of Seat Knott before dropping to ford Bram Rigg Beck near a sheepfold. It continues to climb the Rigg, past another fold and through shallow rocky cuttings to where it eventually gains the ridge just north of the summit. A simple walk over tussocky grass leads to the vicinity of the summit.

I say vicinity of, because Bram Rigg Top seems to have a peripatetic cairn. Well, on my first visit it had no cairn at all while a second visit was greeted with two stones, but in the wrong place. I did something which I had never before done and which I have not repeated: I moved the cairn. It has moved around a bit since then but now seems to be fairly stable. On my last visit I drove a stake through its heart. That may well be the end of it. I shall go back and check.

A short walk to the south-west will regain the main path and take the walker, in less than five minutes, to the fourth of the Howgill tops.

Calders

Calders, 2,211 feet, is the most southern of the Howgill two-thousanders. It is prominent in views from the south and rises to more of a summit than the other, more dome-like Howgill Fells. It must have tricked many walkers into thinking it The Calf, though that higher top is less than a mile to the north and little more climbing is needed to reach it.

I met my brother, one August, on the slopes of Calders. I was staying with my family in Sedbergh; Peter was running in the annual Sedbergh Hills Fell Race,

both unbeknown to the other. I had decided to climb Calders and was halfway up when hordes of, at first dashers, then plodders, then grunters came haring past. Peter was in the middle lot and the surprise was great on both sides. I managed to accompany him to the top where there were people with drinks and walkie-talkies, before he loped off to the far north. It was a cruel race on a very hot, dry day and if the Howgills can be reckoned to be like an outstretched hand then they had to run up and down all the fingers and across the knuckles.

This annual fourteen-mile race involves 6,000 feet of ascent and the winner usually gets round in a couple of minutes over two hours. It finishes in the playing field above the town where blisters and times are compared, equipment in the back of vans assessed, and promises never to do it again, made during lonely ascents on baked fellsides, are forgotten in the bonhomie and in the relief of finishing.

Most visitors to Calders do not run up it but spend a leisurely hour and a half walking up the clear path from Sedbergh which crosses the eastern slopes of Winder and Arant Haw before climbing beside the wire fence to the top. This is a very pleasant route but it can be improved by gaining the watershed on Winder and sticking to the highest ground.

Approaching from the east by way of the path to Cautley Crag, a neat way can be made around the top of the crags before turning to head for Calders across the flat top of Great Dummacks.

A fair-sized cairn marks the top and although the view north is restricted by the plateau of The Calf, that to the south is wide, with the Three Peaks standing in line. Eastwards, across the Rawthey valley, Baugh Fell bulks large.

Once visited, the Howgill Fells cry out to be explored in detail for there is interest in every nook of these rolling hills with their long intervening valleys. A great part of their beauty lies in their immutability. Seasons come and go but these great rounded hills remain, looking down on Bronze Age traveller, Roman legionary, railway navvy and hurrying motorist. There is peace on these empty tops which are spare as the wind and clean as the rain-washed sky.

9
Walking Through Time

Many hill tracks have a history stretching back to droving or mining days. Some are much older and may have been used ever since people first found the need to travel. The best for the walker are those which our present, hectic times have abandoned or half forgotten. The two hills which stand separated by the present Hawes to Buckden road are linked together and traversed by one much older, the Cam High Road. This highway has been followed by Roman legionaries and stagecoach drivers and at present by Pennine Wayfarers and hang glider enthusiasts. Climbing from Ingleton up to Ribblehead and then leaving the B6255 just by Gearstones, the High Road makes its way to Cam End and then behaves like a true Roman road, heading straight as a die towards the first hill of the duo described here.

Dodd Fell

Dodd Fell, 2,192 feet, lies just off the Pennine watershed though its southern slopes still manage to feed both the Ribble and Wharfe, both of which rise near the farm of Cam Houses. This was once a settlement of several farms which in its heyday contained a schoolroom. At the end of the eighteenth century there were a dozen or so families and a domestic style of architecture can be identied in a number of buildings now used as barns. In the High Road's heyday a gun was fired here at nightfall to guide travellers. The farm is now occupied again, after a break during the 1980s and one of the barns has been made into a bunkhouse. This is well sited for walkers as it lies on the Dales Way and is only half a mile from the Pennine Way.

All waters draining off the northern slopes flow into Wensleydale by way of deeply cut Snaizeholme Beck, Little Ing Gill or Duerley Beck.

On the First Series 1:50000 Ordnance Survey Wensleydale and Wharfedale map, the summit of Dodd Fell was honoured with a viewpoint symbol, one of a dozen shown on the sheet. The revised Second Series map of Wensleydale and upper Wharfedale, which covers the same area, only has one viewpoint and that's not on Dodd Fell. Why did the Ordnance Survey have such a change of mind? Possibly it is because many of them were on fell summits – Ingleborough, Whernside, Penyghent, Great Knoutberry Hill – and although the view might be good it cannot always be guaranteed. Or maybe the remoteness of one or two of the viewpoints was thought to be too much of an invitation to the unwary or unprepared. The only one now shown on the map can be driven to.

Anyone who visits Dodd Fell's summit, either expecting it to be a viewpoint or not, will find a trig point standing in a pond in the middle of a fairly damp area. The view is not very good anyway, as the top is too flat and the cairn on Ten End a mile or so further north is far superior. I'll wager the Ordnance Survey man never checked the view before he drew his little blue sun symbol on the map in the first place!

The Ordnance pillar carries the benchmark plaque S5735. On one visit the local farmer's lad was throwing his trail bike up and down a few peat hags while checking on stock, a neat combination of business and pleasure.

The summit has certainly been used as a viewpoint in the distant past for a section of the Roman Road between Ingleton and Bainbridge is perfectly sighted along a straight line between the top and the fort at Bainbridge. For several miles, across the slopes of Drumaldrace to the east, the alignment is followed precisely. On the western side the road follows closely a further alignment between the summit and Cam End for a couple of miles up to Kidhow Gate. A ruler, a pencil and an OS map can provide hours of fun on a rainy day!

Cam High Road remained an important route and in the eighteenth century was known as the Devil's Causeway. The section of road over Cam End and Kidhow, just south of Dodd Fell, was incorporated into the turnpike between Richmond and Lancaster. Authorised in June 1751, it was the main road until 1795 when a deviation was made which is still followed by the present route from Bainbridge to Hawes and then up Widdale to Newby Head before descending to Gearstones near Ribblehead.

In its prime Cam High Road carried a great amount and variety of goods including "quantities of grocery goods, liquors, timber, mahogany and various other articles from Lancaster". Nowadays it's mostly rucksacks and "Wainwrights". The road is tarred from where it leaves the Hawes-Buckden road as far as Cam Houses, thus making the ascent of Dodd Fell nothing more than a gentle stroll from Kidhow Gate. It is best to follow the Pennine Way along West Cam Road for a quarter of a mile or so as far as the gate through the wall.

Few Pennine Wayfarers pass the finger-post at Kidhow Gate, a mile south-west of Dodd Fell's summit, without sitting down for a couple of minutes. It marks the passage from Ribblesdale to Wensleydale and from the Cam High Road to West Cam Road, an old pack-horse route naturally paved with limestone in places. Pack-horses lingered long in this part of Yorkshire, for before the Hawes branch was opened in 1878, the town was sixteen miles from the nearest station. Handloom weaving also continued in this district and pieces were transported to Settle by pack trains over the fells. They would return with weft and warp.

Resting by the cairn on Ten End, it is not difficult to imagine a file of pack-horses making its way across the flank of Dodd Fell, its progress, even in misty weather, marked by the clop of hooves and the tinkling of bells.

Two Roman miles to the north-east, across the valley of Duerley Beck, stands the second of this pair of hills.

Drumaldrace

Drumaldrace, 2,014 feet, vies with its neighbour for the title of easiest Yorkshire two-thousander. Its summit lies not much more than a mile from the junction of the minor road between Hawes and Buckden with the Cam High Road. The height to be gained is a mere 240 feet. Mind, on one occasion the top was only reached after a battle through snowdrifts along the track and it was easy to see why this way was abandoned as the principal road between Richmond and Lancaster, in favour of the present valley route.

Time and again the old ways are the high ways for when people first needed to travel and trade the dales were still forest-bound and boggy.

After three-quarters of a mile the wall on the uphill side peters out and the summit can be reached past some shake holes. A cairn standing in a grassy area marks the top. Ingleborough may just be seen peering over Dodd Fell's shoulder and it is worth walking a few yards north to catch the broadening views of Great Shunner Fell, Mallerstang and the Howgills.

Drumaldrace is a lovely name but it is properly given only to the summit. The hill is Wether Fell, a far more meaningful name, to farmers at least. A wether is a castrated ram. Other animal names on the hill include Marsett Cow Pasture and Cow Stand Gill. Bear Head, east of the summit is presumably a corruption from Bardale which it overlooks rather than a reference to the animal. This valley, the southern boundary of the fell, is rather bleak. Bardale Beck rises in the mire of Fleet Moss on the watershed between Wensleydale and Langstrothdale.

Apart from its agricultural uses, Drumaldrace has, like so many fells, been exploited in the past for its minerals. Old stone quarries abound on the slopes above Gayle and Burtersett and 15,000 tons of stone flags a month were once sent out through Hawes station. There are the pits and shafts of the former Storth Colliery at 1,400 feet beside the Hawes road and lead levels on the lower north-eastern slopes by Burtersett.

The easiest route to Drumaldrace has already been described but the best way is to follow the Roman road, a four-mile march from Bainbridge.

The fort, *Virosidum*, the high seat, stood at the meeting place of the road to Ingleton and one to Ilkley. The former, the Cam High Road as it became, follows the grain of the land and so is everyone's idealised straight Roman road, but the route to *Olicanum* had to make the crossing from Wensleydale to Wharfedale and pursues a much more crooked course.

Leaving the fort, built on a natural hillock south of the confluence of the River Bain with the Ure, the route is surfaced for half a mile or so until, at a sharp left-hand bend, the modern road turns to descend to Countersett. The Roman road strides on, steadily climbing over Bainbridge High Pasture and Common Allotments, walled on each side and displaying a fifteen-foot wide agger, a slight rise on which the road ran and which helped drainage.

Below the summit of Drumaldrace the road reached its maximum altitude, straddling the 1,900-foot contour and running over a bare limestone pavement in places. South-west of Drumaldrace the road is followed by the present minor road between Hawes and Buckden for nearly half a mile. It then heads off towards Kidhow Gate and Cam Fell before dropping down to Ribblehead and Ingleton.

A third approach to Drumaldrace follows an old track from Burtersett over the High Pasture and past the buttress of Yorburgh.

Both its name and its location astride the Roman road give Drumaldrace an air of antiquity but it is not altogether based in the past. A sign on a gate informs members of the Yorkshire Dales Hang Gliding Club that this is a "sensitive site" and tells them where they may take off from. The legionaries, with their fondness for the eagle, would have liked the idea of hang gliding.

10
Of Monks and Shepherds

Place-names are often descriptive and there are many examples in the area bounded by a box of minor roads between Arncliffe (eagle's cliff) and Stainforth (stony ford). This twenty-mile thread of tarmac, a fine route for cyclists, encloses an area of high ground which tops 2,000 feet on the summits of Darnbrook Fell and Fountains Fell. The former name is a description, meaning the hidden stream, and although the latter sounds as if it ought to be, in an area of typical Yorkshire Dales geology, it does not refer to springs at the base of the limestone. Fountains Fell got its name from history, not geography.

Fountains Fell

Fountains Fell, 2,192 feet, was named after the white-cowled Cistercian monks who were granted vast estates in Yorkshire and who had founded Fountains Abbey in 1132. At the height of their landholding, the monks of Fountains had control of about a million acres in the Yorkshire Pennines.

As today, the population of the valleys around Fountains Fell was small so the brothers would have wielded great power over a time span of nearly four centuries. The area owned by the abbey was too large to administer centrally and so a series of granges was planted. One was at Kilnsey on Mastiles Lane, one of the great delights of Yorkshire for walkers, which was part of a route linking the monastic estates from Fountains Abbey, running south of Fountains Fell as Henside Lane and on to other farms and land near another Grange, in Borrowdale in the Lake District.

Sometime after 1150, the grange at Kilnsey was established as a kind of monastic outpost where one of two monks would administer the work of lay brothers and other local labour in running the great sheepwalks which were the economic basis for this part of the abbey's domain.

In one year, around the turn of the fourteenth century, Fountains Abbey exported 76 sacks of wool to Florentine merchants. This may not sound a great deal until it is understood that each sack weighed 364 pounds, making a total of over 12⅓ tons of wool.

The flocks were brought down to Kilnsey from the fells to be sheared and the wool carried thence in wagons to the abbey. The area was divided into farms held by tenants and in summer the shepherds would live in huts on the fells with their sheep.

A sub-grange at Malham looked after the area described here, including the two summits and a large part of what was Gnoup Forest. Gnoup (or Knipe) means a steep place and was the original, descriptive name for Fountains Fell. There were wild red deer here until the beginning of the seventeenth century and abbey records mention wolves being killed as late as the fifteenth.

At the dissolution of the monastery, in 1539, the fell and surrounding areas were bought by Sir Richard Gresham and later came into the possession of Lord Ribblesdale and then the Morrison estate.

Although sheep farming was, and is, the prime economic activity on the fell, it was not the only one, for Fountains Fell Colliery worked two main seams under the summit from about the end of the eighteenth century. Shallow bell pits exploited the 2ft 6in summit seam and a fenced shaft can be seen which went down to the 2ft 4in seam at the base of the millstone grit. Five more seams were not worked as they are only about four inches thick. At its peak of production, which seems to have been the decade between Trafalgar and Waterloo, the pit was selling 900 to 1,000 tons annually. This translates into about 10,000 pack-horse loads a year and it is not surprising that a road was built down to New Pasture on the Arncliffe to Malham road.

This route is now followed by Pennine Wayfarers, some of whom carry packs which would not disgrace a galloway, from above the farm of Tennant Gill where a friendly bull and several of his inquisitive progeny keep an eye on passers-by. The coal road led to Malham for the lead smelt mill, whose chimney still stands half a mile south-west of the tarn, must have been a good customer for most of the nineteenth century. It closed in 1910. You can still pick up bits of coal on the top of the fell. It is hard and shiny and burns with a cheery flame.

The summit also carries an early coke oven, a twelve-foot-square building with an igloo-like interior. It was designed to produce coke for zinc smelting experiments but apparently without success. There is a way in on the north side of the structure which would make a decent enough bivvy.

Walkers who follow the old coal road up from the vicinity of Tennant Gill will arrive near the summit by two stone men close to the wall which runs across the highest ground. There are also two fenced shafts and a host of shallow-workings in the vicinity. The Pennine Way crosses over a stile in the wall and descends steeply along a grooved track which served the colliery from the north. It zigs its way across the steepest ground before following a wall down to the minor road between Halton Gill and Stainforth.

It was by a wall outside Tennant Gill, on a warm, close day, that we met a perspiring, confused figure who, apparently ignoring his plethora of maps and guides and a Pennine Way sign, asked us the way over Fountains Fell. Mike and I soon got used to meeting "Colonel Blimp" who appeared at odd times and in odd places over the next few days. He was usually spotted coming from a different direction or could be seen in the next field or valley from that which the Pennine Way followed and was invariably laden down with all the paraphernalia of an army on the march. We finally lost him on Hadrian's Wall, the lure of the legions being stronger than the prospect of the last 70 miles of moor and forest.

Few Pennine Wayfarers, even those without blimpish handicaps, have either the energy or the inclination to drag themselves away from their route to visit the true summit of Fountains Fell so that, even of a busy Way day, it is likely to be deserted. A large, circular cairn stands near the junction of two walls. Early one January, snowbound and crusted with hoar frost, it resembled the base of an igloo that was only waiting, in a frozen tundra landscape, for a few finishing touches and I almost expected a couple of Inuit hunters to come out from behind the wall. Wrapped and cowled, they would have resembled their monkish predecessors. The top of Fountains Fell can be fairly surreal on occasions.

The view is rather limited to the east because of the flat nature of the summit area and the cairns at the top of the Pennine Way track are a better viewpoint for Buckden Pike and Great Whernside. To the north-west Penyghent stands out grandly.

Half a mile to the south, on the other side of the large tarn which is hidden in a fold of the ground, is the lower, southern top which looks higher than the summit when seen from some directions. Nearby is a disused weather station, a skeletal Stevenson Screen and a few paces away is a fine view over Malham Tarn and the head of Airedale. The shallow Fountains Fell Tarn may be the *Suartcombe*, a Norse name meaning black hollow, which was mentioned in a charter of 1206. It is surprisingly extensive for its hilltop site and reflects the passing cloudscape, changing from bright blue to slate grey in an instant. There are a few smaller tarns on the northern side of the summit wall.

Walkers approaching Fountains Fell from the north can leave the Pennine Way route at the first bend and follow the wall up to the top where there is a wall stile. A patch of scree below the summit is home to a multitude of rabbits which were scurrying about among the rocks on a bright late August day. I approached one which was so studiously involved in nibbling the close grass that I'm sure I could have just leapt on it. A nine-inch hole and a darkly descending tunnel in the middle of the scree rash seemed to point to something bigger than just rabbits being in residence.

It is possible to ascend Fountains Fell from the south, leaving the bridlepath, part of the old route between Arncliffe and Langcliffe, and climbing over Knowe Fell to the southern top. A flint axe head was found on Knowe Fell, indicating that trade was carried on between eastern England and Yorkshire back in Neolithic times.

With a name rooted in the Middle Ages and an interesting economic past, Fountains Fell certainly has history on its side. Although it displays a less striking shape when compared with some of its neighbours, it also has a claim to geographical fame for it is the southernmost 2,000-foot summit in Yorkshire.

Darnbrook Fell

Darnbrook Fell, 2,047 feet, has, at first sight, little of any sort of claim to fame. It occupies the eastern end of the high ground between Littondale and the two roads out of that valley towards the west. Its western boundary is chiefly formed by the 'hidden stream' after which it is named and which rises in the col between the two fells. From this peaty depression Darnbrook Beck flows south-eastwards to join Cowside Beck below Nab End.

Darnbrook House was a tenant farm of Fountains Abbey from the twelfth century but was no doubt a pastoral farm from much earlier; certainly the name of the next habitation along the road to Malham, Thoragill Beck House, demonstrates its Norse origins.

The most usual way to visit Darnbrook Fell is as part of a walk over Fountains Fell using the Pennine Way. The lower summit is reached by following the wall between the two tops. A stile has been built over the wall at the Fountains Fell end. It is best to keep with the wall for any diversion from it brings the walker into some of the many deep peat groughs below the summit. A plantation is growing south of the wall, where some of Darnbrook Beck's headwaters rise.

Another approach follows the wall which leaves the old monastic track from Litton across Cow Close and Dawson Close. The wall leaves the track where it crosses a stream above an area of limestone. This is a delightful walk, as is the whole of the deep cleft of the valley of Penyghent Gill which it follows around the north side of the fell from Nether Hesleden to Giant's Grave, the remains of a barrow of the late Neolithic age. The limestone gill abounds with flowers in spring and early summer and the lower slopes are peppered with rabbit burrows. The footbridge marked on the Ordnance map is no longer in existence and no right-of-way follows the stream, though there is one on the far side between the road and Nether Hesleden and this gives good views down into the valley with its scars separated by green shelves. A limekiln and the mouth of Snorkel Cave are prominent, as are the rectangular enclosures of early settlements.

The summit, which is marked by a trig point (S5618) standing on a square plinth, is fairly flat and the view is restricted, though Penyghent looks commanding, more so from the edge of the plateau than from the top itself.

Darnbrook Fell descends broadly to the south-east over West Moor whose eastern slopes hold what is arguably the fell's best feature, Scoska Cave. The entrance is large and the cave continues, rectangular in section and about six feet high for over 50 yards before it divides. The right-hand passage, narrower than the entrance, can be followed for a further 100 yards or so, gradually lowering into a crawl.

After a walk on the rather bleak top of Darnbrook Fell, the spirits can be raised by following the delightful path between Litton and Arncliffe. Littondale runs down to join that most wonderful of Yorkshire valleys, Wharfedale.

Of Monks and Shepherds

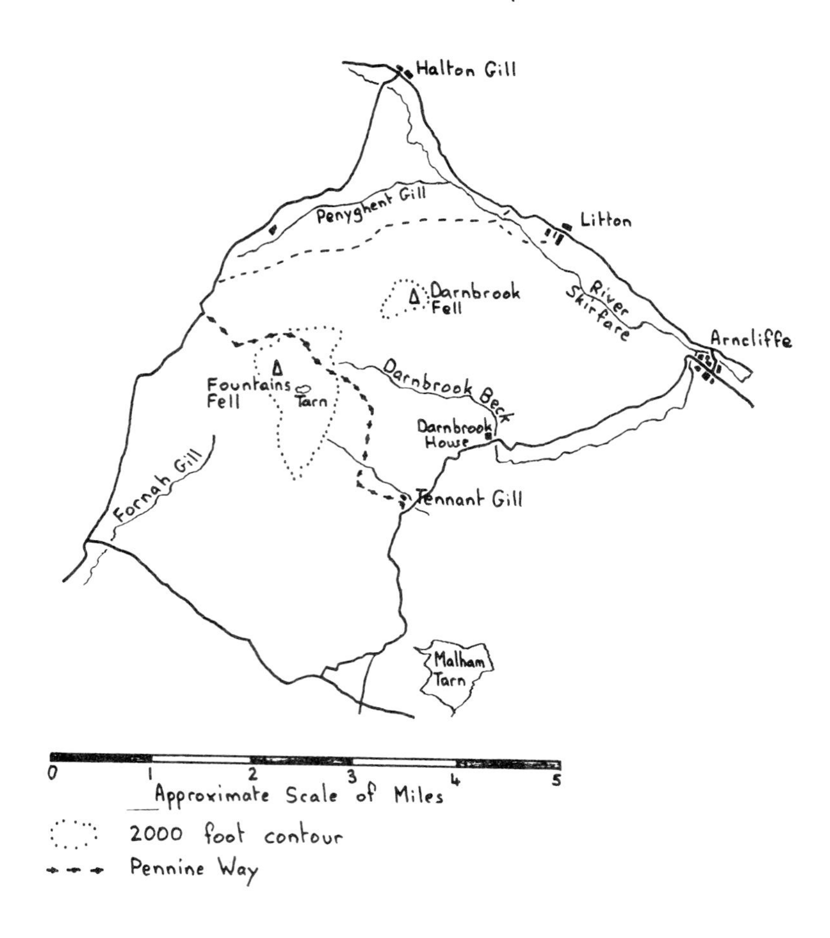

11
Wharfedale Round

The five 2,000-foot tops which stand guard around the upper reaches of this lauded valley can be traversed by a good walker in a day. A sense of achievement and tired limbs are a part of the prize for this excursion of nearly two dozen miles, but the ever-changing glimpses into, and views across, the valley are the real reward, for only over a long distance and a long space of time does the walker truly catch the changing nuances of the scene. To look across the valley to see the rising light picking out a scar and then, hours later, to stand on that scar and look the other way to where the evening sun lights the earlier vantage point is an experience only gained at some expense, but a reward which will never be forgotten.

Having completed the round, though, the walker will have to return many times in order to start to learn something about the hills. Well, that's one excuse!

Great Whernside

Great Whernside, 2,310 feet, is the highest of the fells around Wharfedale and carries the most eastern 2,000-foot top in Yorkshire. It is also a vast hill, planting its feet in Nidderdale and Coverdale as well as in Wharfedale. To drive round Great Whernside, keeping on the nearest public roads to the fell, is a journey of 50 miles.

Much of this huge area is water-gathering ground for the Angram and Scar House reservoirs which serve Bradford and the walker is not particularly welcome. Few rights-of-way cross the ridge which Great Whernside tops and most of these are towards the east, where the high land declines between Nidderdale and Coverdale. The fourteen miles of broad, high ridge between the Grassington-Pateley Bridge road and the top of Little Whernside, five miles beyond the main top, are crossed by just two rights-of-way.

Perhaps the fact that grouse shooting as well as water gathering is important in a large chunk of countryside south-east of the summit helps to explain the situation.

The name comes from the same root as *quern*, indicating that the gritstone was used for the making of millstones, while the prefix was probably a reflection of the fell's bulk rather than its height as it is a hundred feet lower than its better-known namesake. At least one roughed-out millstone can still be found on the northern slopes. *Wharnside Hill* features boldly on Yorkshireman Christopher Saxton's map of 1577.

Millstone grit and water are not the only substances to have been extracted from Great Whernside. Its southern and western slopes saw a good deal of lead mining, particularly above Grassington and around Dowber Gill, and there was a smelting mill at Kettlewell.

The lower western slopes of the fell, underlain by limestone, are very rich in the remains of the settlements, field systems and homesteads carved out by the early pastoralists who first settled this area, on the sweet land between the boggy valley and the wet uplands.

Just north of Grassington, where the remains are most extensive, medieval

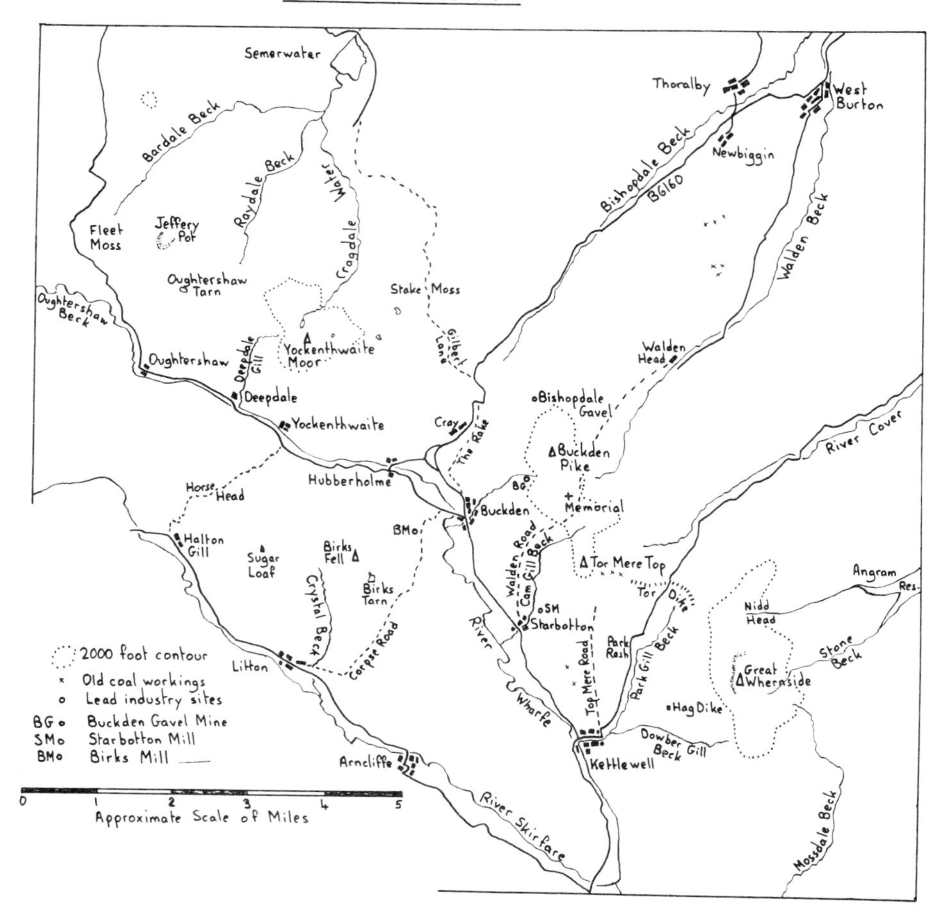

fields overlie older ones which date back to Romano-British times or earlier. Here, small square or rectangular fields stretch up the hillside, precursors of the much larger enclosures which now spread their walls up the slope. Several small farmsteads and rectangular huts have been identified as well as tracks and pathways, and there is burial evidence of settlement from the Bronze Age.

Although they are not as thick on the ground further north, there are field systems and enclosures above Kettlewell, overlooked by Great Whernside and passed by the walker who approaches the summit from the village.

There may be a dearth of routes across the fell but there is certainly no lack of rights-of-way from Kettlewell on to the lower western slopes. With two footpaths and two bridleways, the walker is spoiled for choice.

The most direct way heads across fields to the north of Dowber Gill Beck to the former farm of Hag Dike, now an outdoor centre for scouts, while a bridleway makes a more circuitous journey to the same destination, using the farm road to Hay Tonge for the first part of its route. Another path follows the north bank of Dowber Gill Beck, leading to the site of the Providence lead mine, passing the manhole cover entrance to the pothole of the same name. There are extensive tips at the mine and a waterwheel pit and crushing floor stand up the hillside above the path. The fourth track, now a bridleway and formerly the mine road, goes past Rain Slack Well to fizzle out in a damp area near an old coal shaft. A further path follows the top of the intake wall southwards to join up with the Conistone Turf Road and this makes a pleasant walk for a day when the tops seem too far away.

Hag Dike stands at over 1,500 feet and dates from a late eighteenth-century time of great agricultural optimism. Few farms were built this high in Yorkshire in historic times for the land is so marginal that a succession of good years could hardly be hoped for, let alone expected.

The former farm stands on the most important of Yorkshire Dales boundaries. More important than that of the national park following the high ground around the head of Nidderdale and which passes the summit, it is the oldest boundary and it marks the change from rock to rock. Whichever path is followed from Kettlewell, the walk so far has been a delight over springy turf speckled with flowers. At Hag Dike everything changes. Limestone gives way, first to the Yoredales (not as thick here as, say, on Ingleborough) and then the millstone grit which underlies the moors for a great area and which makes Nidderdale such a good water-catchment area.

When the limestone is left behind the flora, soil, colour tones, the whole mood of the landscape alters. Springy green turf, dotted with wild flowers gives way to cotton-grass and tussocks. Even the path changes and the walker soon discovers if his boots are waterproof. If the Brontës had lived in this part of Yorkshire instead of Haworth, they would have lived at Hag Dike, not Hay Tonge.

The way to the top from Hag Dike seems long but the reward justifies the effort.

The extensive, flat summit is littered with large blocks of millstone grit which look as if they have been tipped from some giant wheelbarrow and the top itself carries a large cairn and a trig point with the benchmark number 2976. There is plenty of shelter among the boulders and crag and it is often needed. The view is wide-ranging on a good day though the best glimpses down into Nidderdale are gained by walking north a mile to Nidd Head.

There is neither a wall nor a fence along Great Whernside's broad summit ridge until the wall running up from the top of the Kettlewell-Coverdale road is met at Black Dike End near Nidd Head. From here there is a good view down into Nidderdale and Bradford's communal baths. The reservoirs came on tap in 1913 and 1936 and the construction was assisted by a light railway which also served the scattered inhabitants of upper Nidderdale. It was run by Bradford Corporation until 1929 and dismantled in 1936.

The ridge wall swings round to the north-east and on a minor top just beyond Nidd Head there is a large boundary stone in the wall inscribed YB on the path side and KB on the other. It then runs on over Little Whernside (1,984 feet), Dead Man's Hill and Great Haw, where it divides. Rights-of-way run from near Great Haw down into Coverdale and Nidderdale.

At one time the most popular route up Great Whernside ran from the top of the road to the wall corner on the ridge but this was never a right-of-way and walkers are encouraged to use the bridleway, part of an old route between Starbotton and Nidderdale, which climbs diagonally from the road summit to the col between Great and Little Whernside.

This track, which may be of monastic origin and which was certainly used by pack-horses, runs in a slight depression on the upper slopes and is very wet in places. On the Nidderdale side it descends to the ruins of the former hunting lodge and inn at Lodge where it meets another track crossing the eastern slopes

On Great Whernside

"THA wants ta knaw t'way t'Whernside, dost tha? Ah've niver bin aboov Bycliff. T'will be roof waaking. If tha gits t'top ther'ull be nowt but 'eap o' stanes."

Thus spoke a gaunt dalesman, landlord of the inn at Hebden that stands on the time-worn pack-horse road which straddles the fells. Many times since then I have walked the trackless solitudes of Great Whernside, but my first impression is still the sharpest etched; remembered too as the only time when I have met another wanderer in that wilderness.

Early one morning, at the very climax of a sweltering summer, I climbed up Hebden Ghyll, passed the derelict lead mines, and came to that lonely dwelling, Ghyll House, grey and stark under Blackedge; stone walls alone prevent the moorland from engulfing it. Sun-scorched, I toiled over Conistone Moor and floundered into that black area of peat hags which guards the massive flank of Whernside. I staggered over the shaky hummocks of tussock grass to slither down the slimy sides into boggy deeps, some fifteen feet below.

When I at last emerged to the wide horizon of the rocky slope which rises to the summit, a vast thundercloud, white-capped with towered cumulus, shrouded Hawkswick Clowder. Then, too, I heard the warning indrawn sigh of airs wandering among the dry coarse grass.

Over chaotic rocks I reached the cairns and rested. Wharfedale brimmed with a wall of cloud which opened to chasms of flaming copper as lightning struck to earth.

Suddenly I heard the grating of nailed boots on granite. A young man, sack on shoulders, sheep-dog at heel, passed. He pointed towards Kettlewell and his lips were moving, but the words were lost in the roar of thunder. I got up and followed him as with long strides he swung down the rough fell-side. Blinded with sweat I plunged after him over tussocks, peat and walls, at length splashing down a water-course to reach the street of Kettlewell and the fireside of an inn. After the storm we parted, he to his home, I to the long road back to Hebden.

A day or two later the inn-keeper there hailed me — "So tha foound t'way t'top. Tom Grassby cam t'pub Saturday an' tauld 'ow 'e met one fra Loondon. I reckoned it wad be you."

Thereafter they received me into the trusty brotherhood of those who walk their fells.

W.C.H. King
(The Yorkshire Dalesman, December 1946)

of Little Whernside below Dead Man's Hill. In 1728 three headless corpses were found buried here, probably the remains of Scottish pedlars who had gone missing some years before. The bodies had been preserved by the peat in which they were buried.

Great Whernside is usually climbed from the west, but for the strong walker there is a sixteen-mile round tour from the east, following rights-of-way except for the stretch along the summit ridge. A footpath from Middlesmoor descends across fields to How Stean Beck before climbing past Low Riggs and High Riggs on to the fellside. It parallels How Stean Beck across a grouse moor and then follows Straight Stean Beck to gain the ridge, north-west of the round top of Meugher, at Sandy Gate. Boundary stones and cairns mark the route to the summit, at first north-west over Blake Hill to a subsidiary top which just reaches 2,000 feet, the most easterly such height in Yorkshire. Here the way turns westwards before swinging round again to north-north-west and the summit.

The return journey follows the ridge round to where the old track down to Lodge runs off on the right. The Carle Fell Road is picked up and Scar House dam crossed before In Moor Lane, an enclosure road, runs across another grouse moor back to Middlesmoor.

This is a tough walk and the miles seem long. It is also a rewarding one for the walker who enjoys solitude. A spring day with the skylarks singing and with cumulus clouds billowing along through a bright sky enlivens the scene which, in the upper reaches of the valley at least, has the austerity which public works always bring to the landscape.

The wall which descends from the summit ridge follows, for the last half-mile to the road, Tor Dike, a linear mound with a deep ditch at its foot, built in prehistoric times and later used to enclose a deer park set up early in the fifteenth century. Across the road Tor Dike continues along the side of a broad fell which manages to thrust itself up above the 2,000 foot contour.

Tor Mere Top

Tor Mere Top, 2,050 feet, is the middle and lowest of the three tops forming the eastern boundary of Wharfedale. It rises steeply above Starbotton and descends very gradually north-eastwards, the high ground undulating to throw up the lesser tops of Brown Haw, Harland Hill and the instantly recognisable Penhill, before the ridge peters out above West Witton in Wensleydale.

Coverdale and the Walden Beck valley form its dip slope borders while Park Gill Beck and Cam Gill Beck separate Tor Mere Top from Great Whernside and Buckden Pike on the Wharfedale side.

Cam Gill Beck, which gathers its water from the slopes of Tor Mere Top and Buckden Pike, once nearly destroyed the village at its foot, for a storm on the fellside in June 1686 gave rise to a violent flood which surged down the constricted valley. Houses in Starbotton were washed away or filled with stones and gravel up to their bedroom windows. Pasture land was covered with gravel and mud and the bridge swept away. We may think of disaster relief as a modern phenomenon but the seventeenth-century records show much generosity. The inhabitants of Leathley, 30 miles down Wharfdale, collected nine shillings and fourpence for "ye poore and distressed Inhabitants of Kettlewell and Starbotton – who suffered by a dreadful inundation of water", while in faraway Cambridgeshire the villagers of Trumpington sent nearly half that amount "for loss by an earthquake at Kettlewell, Yorkshire".

The summit can be visited most easily from the top of the Kettlewell –

Wensley road above Park Rash. This involves a walk of about a mile and a climb of only 400 feet and would suit the visitor with only an hour or so to spare. The more usual way of tackling Tor Mere Top is as part of a walk to all three summits from Kettlewell, a good day's walk for most folk. The best way is to use the Top as an excuse to explore some of the old roads which grace this part of Wharfedale.

There is, of course, a good historical reason for the development of such a dense network of tracks. Kettlewell was the market centre for upper Wharfedale before Grassington became more important. The major local medieval land-owners, Fountains Abbey, Coverham Abbey and Bolton Priory, had interests here as did the Nevilles of Middleham Castle. In the eighteenth and nineteenth centuries lead mining brought increasing pack-horse traffic and there was always the local need for fuel from the fellside.

Tor Mere Road, a wide green track, walled for much of its length, heads straight up the fellside above Kettlewell to Cam Head where it meets the Starbotton Cam Road. One of the reasons for the tracks is apparent from the map, for Starbotton Peat Ground is shown just south of Tor Mere Top. The Kettlewell peat ground was also around the summit. Coal and lead were mined on Tor Mere Top, though the lead mines were small-scale affairs compared with others in the vicinity and were not the main customers of the smelting mill which stood beside Cam Gill Beck, north-east of Kettlewell.

The mill started work around the end of the seventeenth century, mainly to deal with ore from the mines around Dowber Gill, and was largely rebuilt in 1868 when a long flue was built to a high chimney at nearly 1,200 feet on the side of the Cam. Top Mere Road passes the site of the chimney and its base can be seen, together with the arched stone flue. The mill itself was demolished by the military in 1942 while testing a new kind of explosive. It was obviously very efficient.

The flue and chimney were built in response to many complaints about the injurious effect that fumes from the smelter were having on cattle. The men who cleaned out the soot which could be re-smelted for its lead content got four shillings a shift.

The mill used peat from the fell and Ralph Place, agent for the Old Providence Mining Co. in 1867, wrote: "I think peat is not only the best material for smelting, but is much cheaper than anything else." However, there were supply problems and it seems that the mining companies supplied the smelter with peat. The latter's owner, the Manor of Kettlewell, seemed reluctant to pay too generous a price for its fuel, for in 1871, Place wrote again: "To the Trust Lords of the Manor of Kettlewell, on behalf of the Providence Mining Co. I am instructed to inform you that they are willing to continue supplying fuel to the mill....We find 7/- per ton don't pay for the trouble attending it.."

Standing on Top Mere Road now, looking down on Kettlewell and the narrow pastoral stretch of Wharfedale below it, it is difficult to imagine the smelter chimney billowing smoke, loads of peat being brought down the track, men walking up to the pits near the summit and donkeys carrying coal down on their backs.

Descending the road one February, after a visit to the summit, I found it completely full of snow and passable only along a narrow trampled track down one side. The pastures on either hand were almost completely free of snow.

Tor Mere Top's summit lies just west of the wall running along the ridge and consists of a small cairn. The wall is precarious and is surmounted by a two-strand wire fence and walkers following the path on the other side should be content to look over at the cairn. There is little height difference between the cairn and the foot of the wall anyway.

Anyone who must visit the cairn at all costs should approach by way of the bridleway which links Starbotton Cam Road with the Walden Road, as this runs through the enclosure on Starbotton Out Moor which contains the summit.

The walk from Kettlewell to the summit via Top Mere Road, descending along Starbotton Cam Road and returning to the starting point through the fields between the two villages is a journey, literally, through Paradise. If you don't believe me, look at your map!

The 1½-mile walk along the watershed to the next summit may not seem quite so heavenly, but as A.J. Brown wrote in *Broad Acres:* "Toiling up the Pike, a man feels but a puny thing on the face of the earth, but walking 'ower 't tops', he takes on a giant stature."

Buckden Pike

Buckden Pike, 2,303 feet, is a more compact fell than its near neighbour Great Whernside and has a friendlier feel about it. Rising above the valley of the bucks, for this area was part of Lanstrothdale Chase in the days when the Percys of Northumberland were the feudal lords, the Pike played an important part in the shaping of the landscape before there were deer, or indeed names, hereabouts.

In glacial times, ice moving eastwards from the high ground of Langstrothdale Chase was channelled north or south by Buckden Pike. The southern ice carved out Wharfedale's glorious glacial trough while the northern flow moved over the col above Cray and went down Bishopdale. The steepness of the upper part of the dale speeded up the flow of the glacier to such an extent that a deep U-shaped valley was gouged out. In fact, such was the deepening that Wensleydale hangs to its tributary Bishopdale, Aysgarth Falls on the main valley being witness to the Ure's attempts to catch up.

Buckden Pike protected the Walden valley on its east side from the erosive force of the ice and so that valley still retains its pre-glacial V-shaped profile. The top of the Pike was high enough to remain above the level of the glaciers, its summit not being covered with ice.

It is now covered in peat, thanks to the underlying beds of millstone grit, and it fairly wet in places, especially in the dip between the summit and Tor Mere Top.

In the 1880s there were proposals to tunnel under Buckden Pike for a railway which was to join Wharfedale and Wensleydale. This was to be a continuation of the line from Skipton to Threshfield and would pass through Kettlewell and Buckden before leaving upper Wharfedale though the tunnel which was to emerge in Bishopdale, after 1¼ miles underground, to join the North Eastern Railway's Wensleydale branch west of Aysgarth station. Like several other fanciful schemes to build railways through Wharfedale, including one with a 6,000-yard tunnel under Great Whernside, the Skipton and Kettlewell (Extension to Aysgarth) Bill was thrown out by Parliament, and the line got no further up the dale than Threshfield.

The only tunnels to have actually been constructed under the fell are those dug in connection with lead mining. There were two main sites on the fell and remains can be seen at both. To the north of the summit, Bishopdale Gavel was worked by opencuts and shafts driven down through the millstone grit. The principal mine, Buckden Gavel, lying south-west of the summit, was worked at first by bell pits and shafts but the remoteness and height of the workings, above

2,000 feet in places, led to the construction of a level near the head of Buckden Beck. Seven feet high and four feet wide, transport was by tubs on iron rails. Three hundred and thirty fathoms in three veins ere cut which provided ore to keep the mine working for many years. Dressing floors were built at the portal and the ore was carried along a new road across Buckden East Side Pasture to be smelted at Low Mill on Cam Gill at Starbotton.

This route makes a fine line of approach to Buckden Pike for it is well graded, gaining height gradually across the enclosures above Eshber Wood and then following the edge of a spur of the fell round and up to the level mouth. Although virtually blocked with stones, the arch, finely wrought and with an inscribed keystone, is an evocative memorial to the men who worked here a century and a half ago virtually under the summit of the Pike. This is especially so on a day of low cloud when sound is stifled and sight confused and the dressing floors and level portal loom unexpectedly out of the mist.

A monument of a very different kind stands on the summit ridge half a mile south of the top of the Pike, but one which is even more startling to the unprepared visitor. A marble cross, standing on a plinth of the slabby local gritstone, stands in memory of five Polish R.A.F. airmen who died when their Wellington bomber crashed here in a blizzard at the end of January 1942. It was erected 31 years later by the only survivor who had stumbled from the wreckage into the storm on that bleak fell top. After wandering for some time, he realised by the surrounding desolation that he was unlikely to reach any habitation and so began to retrace his footsteps towards the wreck. On the way back his footsteps crossed those of a fox and by a happy chance the airman decided to follow them. The tracks led to a stream and the stream to the hamlet of Cray.

It was soon discovered that the survivor had been wandering about on the fell with a broken leg.

Ironically, another war-plane came down on this mountain 44 years to the month after the Wellington. An R.A.F. Phantom crashed into Walden Moor only a mile or so north-east of the monument after the two fliers had ejected to safety. The area was immediately closed by the authorities while a search was carried out for all the "sensitive" bits and pieces scattered across the fellside.

One of the delights of Buckden Pike is the number of waterfalls tumbling down its western side. These occur when streams cross the step-like strata of the Yoredale rocks and they make an attractive contribution to the scenery and sound of the hillside. One such fall is on Cow Close Gill above Cray and when a westerly gale is blowing the water is thrown high into the air forming a plume of spray above the scar. We visited the fall on a day when more water seemed to be going up than down while a quartet of horses galloped around the pasture.

There are ways to the top of the Pike to suit every taste. Buckden Beck's deeply entrenched gill points straight at the summit with the bonus of a visit to the Buckden Gavel level. Above the level an old wall continues to the summit ridge about a third of a mile south of the trig point.

Two more tracks converge at the level entrance, the one from Starbotton already mentioned and a further, earlier mine track which was built to join Buckden Rake in the days when ore was taken from the mine to be smelted across the Wharfe at Birks Mill.

The Rake itself, climbing around the Pike's western slopes from the car park in the village to join the modern B6160 Bishopdale road at Cray High Bridge, is a delight every yard of the way if rude messages from farmers are ignored. In its lower stages through Rakes Wood it is on a ledge of limestone which has been artificially cut out in some places. Higher up, above the wood, The Rake runs

Buckden Pike in wartime

I SET out to climb Buckden Pike as a prelude to the day. There are, of course, several ways of climbing the Pike; the approach I like best starts from Cray and leads straight up the steepest shoulder, but this time I followed the green track which starts from Buckden, crosses the beck and ascends the hill by easy stages.

When I reached the lower woods I turned round for a last look at the village and the valley. There was something peculiarly satisfying about those grey stone farms and cottages; something reassuring about the way the blue smoke curled from the chimneys; and something so solid and durable about the whole village that was singularly comforting. It was the best answer I had seen to the fulminations of the dictators: and the vaunted strength of the Siegfried Line. For how many wars have devastated Europe since Buckden first appeared on the scene and how little it has changed through the centuries. This war may be different from all the preceding wars, but I fancy Buckden will look precisely the same when the tumult and the shouting dies again, and the men march back.

When I reached the summit of the Pike, a snell wind was blowing from the east, but the air was so invigorating that I had a mind to spend the day on the tops rather than to descend to one of the neighbouring valleys. There is nothing spectacular about the Pike itself; it is just a shaggy giant of the early world — a great lump of a mountain — but the view from the top is enchanting. The long line of the Pennines unfolds itself to the view. Penyghent, Fountains Fell, Ingleborough and the three Whernsides tower above the surrounding fells, and the Lakeland mountains pile up in the west.

Toiling up the Pike, a man feels but a puny thing on the face of the earth, but walking "ower t'tops" he takes on giant stature. Down in the valley one examines the landscape microscopically; one picks out the contrasting greens and browns and greys, the little becks and gills, and all the things which go to make a beautiful scene. But up on the tops, everything is seen on the grand scale: whole dales and forests: far-flung ridges and toppling hills: masses of rock and limestone: great vistas of cloudy sky; and everywhere long straggling walls that seem to go sheer up the fellsides to the far horizons.

Alfred J. Brown
(The Yorkshire Dalesman, January 1940)

very straight along a gently climbing limestone terrace and it comes as no surprise to learn that this is a section of the Roman road running between the forts at Ilkley and Bainbridge.

Another old track, this time a pack-horse route between Wharfedale and Wensleydale, can be followed from Starbotton to where it crosses the summit ridge to the south-east of the memorial cross. This is the Walden Road and it climbs above the west side of Cam Gill Beck on to Knuckle Bone Pasture. At a bifurcation of the track near an area of old workings above the head of the beck, the left-hand fork should be taken to gain the ridge. Here is a ruined building, thought to be a shelter for the men who led the pack-horse trains over this pass which attains a height of 2,150 feet.

Of course, the Walden Road can be followed from the other side, from where the tarmac ends at Walden Head. A steep section around Deepdale Gill is followed by a gradual climb over Walden Moor and the hasty may be tempted to head straight for the summit from where the track turns south. It is probably better to adopt the steady plod of the pack-horse and follow the track past the remains of Hard Rake quarry to where it tops the ridge by a boundary stone engraved with the letters B and O.

The summit of Buckden Pike is marked by a trig point numbered S5520 and a cairn of the same slabby gritstone which makes up the nearby wall. The latter runs right across the top of the fell and gives good shelter. The trig point on its concrete base stands in a little depression made in the peat by the boots and hoofs of the many, human and ovine, who have walked round it. Being a depression, it generally holds water.

The summit makes a good viewpoint with Ingleborough, Penyghent and Fountains Fell looking bold and inviting away to the west. On the other side of the wall, rolling ridges sweep down to long valleys. There is a pleasing contrast here.

Walkers based in Buckden who follow The Rake and turn their back on the Pike will find their gaze focussed on a large, dumpy fell with well-wooded lower slopes which effectively seals the head of Wharfedale.

Yockenthwaite Moor

Yockenthwaite Moor, 2,110 feet, plants its feet in four valleys: Langstrothdale to the south, Wensleydale to the north, Raydale to the west and Bishopdale to the east, as well as having a toehold in the very head of Wharfedale.

Its highest point is on the moorland north of the Wharfe's pronounced change of direction, between Hubberholme and Buckden, where it throws off the constrictions of Langstrothdale for its broader and tamer mid-section.

Yockenthwaite Moor is not one of the popular fells of the Yorkshire Dales and, with one notable exception, the walker will find a definite lack of paths apart from those around the lowest slopes. It is not easy walking country for its top is broad, badly drained and peaty. In thick weather direction finding can be trying, to say the least.

A good way of exploring much of what the fell has to offer is to follow a round from Buckden. One of the best views of Yockenthwaite Moor is from halfway up The Rake, a section of Roman road which is followed for the first part of the walk. This track joins the B6160 Buckden-Bishopdale road just above Cray High Bridge and follows the road round a sharp bend on to a section called Causeway, sure proof of the antiquity of the road.

At Causeway Moss the tarmac is abandoned and a stony, walled track, Gilbert

Lane, joined. This soon starts to climb, steeply in sections through the bends at Hell Gap, to join the open moor, at about 1,800 feet, on the former North and West Riding boundary near a large gritstone boulder inscribed B4M. At least the walker now knows how far he's just come.

On its way up from the road, Gilbert Lane passes the lumps and mounds which mark the site of an ancient settlement dating back possibly to the Bronze Age. The early pastoralists chose their site well, on a green ledge above a limestone scar and with a nearby spring for a water supply. They would also have enjoyed a fine view across to Buckden Pike.

Although the way to Yockenthwaite Moor abandons the old road where the wall veers off to the right, it is worthwhile making a detour along it for a quarter-mile or so to see where the route crosses the only firm bit of ground, an area of limestone, amid the bleakness of Stake Moss. Lady Anne Clifford crossed this way and was less than impressed.

A westerly walk from the top of the walled section of Gilbert Lane leads to South Grain Tarn in a peaty hollow on the moor. It is an interesting exercise in navigation to try and locate the bell pit which is marked on the map to the north-east of the tarn. It speaks volumes for the desolation of Yockenthwaite Moor that this mere round rash of stones in the midst of peaty surroundings is singled out as a feature. The solitary nature of the pit and the lack of spoil around it indicates that it was not a successful venture. A mere trial, probably for lead, and the passer-by wonders why t'owd men chose this spot.

The rest of the climb up to the summit plateau follows intermittent walls, fences, boundary posts and ditches over Cray Moss. To the north is the narrow tarn of Hunters Hole, though whether he drove his prey towards it or fell into it is not recorded. Eventually the trig point is sighted in the distance and a ten-minute game of hide-and-seek over hags and through groughs ensues before it is reached.

There is no shelter on this bleak summit and in bad weather accurate navigation or a lot of luck is necessary to locate it. A previous visitor, Nick Wright, writing about a 1968 visit, described it as "the most decrepit of trig points". It has obviously had a face lift and at least one coat of whitewash in the past twenty years! Just for the record, the trig point carries benchmark S5500.

It took the writer three attempts before the view from the top could be seen and although the summit area is too flat to give good distant views, for a close-up of acres of wrinkled peat moor, it has few peers in Yorkshire. The Three Peaks appear in line and the Buckden Pike-Great Whernside ridge is well illuminated by early evening sun. Later, as the light fades, swell after swell of fell roll away to the north-west, each one a slightly paler shade of grey, towards the setting sun.

There is a lot of cloudberry on the summit plateau and, north-west of the trig point, an area of old stone pits complete with a well-built square hut which seems to grow out of the rock and which is only lacking a roof.

A walk northwards for half a mile, passing more tarns and more peat, brings the visitor to the small cairn marking the subsidiary top of Cragdale Moor which has plenty of the latter but little of either of the former in its vicinity. This route can be continued further, with numerous changes of direction along the wall which provides a guide for much of the way, past Oughtershaw Tarn to Fleet Moss and the summit of the Hawes to Buckden road at Long Slack Gate. From whichever direction you come along the ridge, Oughtershaw Tarn appears suddenly, as the ground you are walking on, well-drained and springy, drops away to the peaty hollow in which lies the tarn. A wire fence has recently been built across this wet depression, replacing a tumbledown wall. To the north, afforested Raydale leads down to Semerwater while southwards Plover Hill and Fountains Fell stand like twins. To my eye they looked like two destroyers manoeuvring line abreast and the nautical allusion was continued as, nearer to the summit, Penyghent appears to the east of Plover Hill, looking for all the world like the unbalanced superstructure on one side of an aircraft carrier.

Fleet Moss itself is not as fearsome as its name, or the map, might suggest, as a series of drainage channels now seams through it. It is still soggy and peaty, though, and an old fence has given up the ghost. Although it can't be so in such a patently wet area, the fence posts, or what is left of them, look desiccated. From the stile at the eastern end of the moss it is possible to look straight down the gap between Ingleborough and Whernside and see the gas platforms in Morecambe Bay.

To complete the circular walk back to Buckden, though, it is necessary to go south-east from the trig point, down and up some of the wettest, deepest groughs, to a fine wall which can be followed down steeply to the valley of Strans Gill and then to the path leading to Scar House.

The change from barren top to verdant valley is quite striking and whichever branch of the path is followed, either down to Hubberholme and along the Wharfe or around to Cray and back down The Rake, the return is a delight and full of interest.

Place-names make a fascinating study and the environs of Yockenthwaite Moor can tell us something about the history of the place. What names the original settlers, people of the Bronze Age who built the stone circle near the Wharfe to the west of Yockenthwaite and the settlement by Gilbert Lane, gave to their surroundings we cannot know, because features have been renamed by later dwellers.

The biggest place-name legacy is that of the Norse settlers, like the Irish-Viking Eogan whose clearing or thwaite gives us the name of hamlet and fell. Other local Norse names occur at Deepdale Gill, Oughtershaw and Raisgill.

Chapel Moor, high above Scar House, reminds us that Hubberholme church was once a chapel of ease in Arncliffe Parish. To the east and north of the moor New Pasture Allotments and Cragdale Allotments refer, as do High, Middle and Low Pastures above Cray, to the late eighteenth- and early nineteenth-century enclosures of the moorlands. Dry stone walls march straight up the fellsides, marking the land alloted to different farms. Some of them just peter out on the boggy moor top. Perhaps the land was so poor it didn't repay the cost of dividing it or maybe the land was too wet to build on.

Some names tell us of past farming practices stretching back for generations like Cow Pasture and Hay Close, while others such as Stake Moss and Cray Moss are extremely accurate descriptions!

On the walk back to Buckden, the visitor will not fail to be impressed by the steep slope stretching away to the south. This is part of a long ridge of high ground, between Langstroth and Wharfedale on the one hand and Littondale, drained by the Skirfare, on the other, which attains its summit on the last of the high fells around Wharfedale.

Birks Fell

Birks Fell, 2,001 feet. So said the old one-inch map but things have changed. The 1985 1:25,000 Outdoor Leisure map deprives the "summit" of its spot height and replaces it with one on the far side of the wall, but at a height of only approximately 1,995 feet. A higher top is now shown near Sugar Loaf, a mile to the west-north-west of the old "summit", but even this newly predominant height is only just over 1,998 feet.

Perhaps a party of stout-hearted Yorkshire folk will one day construct a cairn high enough to return Birks Fell to the status which the O.S. formerly granted it!

Two thousand feet or not, it still makes a grand walk and can be recommended for the visitor who wants to get a good flavour of the Dales but is limited for time.

There are several ways of climbing Birks Fell as the ridge is crossed by half a dozen rights-of-way. The author's preference is to use the bridleway which runs between Buckden and Litton. This was used as a corpse road in the days when Hubberholme church was but a chapel of ease and Buckden had no church. Burials had to take place at Arncliffe and the journey could be a fraught one. Records tell of a corpse being lost in the flooded Wharfe and of a party of eight corpse bearers almost losing their own lives in snowdrifts.

The track leaves Dubb's Lane, between Buckden and Hubberholme, and climbs through sparse woodland above Redmire farm. The lower, steep slopes of Wharfedale hereabouts are delightful with their mixture of ash, birch and hazel woods and flowery meadows, and the path climbs enticingly to reach the open fellside where Water Gill gurgles and tumbles down to the valley. It was its early covering of birch woodland which gave the fell its name.

A diversion of a couple of hundred yards up the stream brings the visitor to a shooting hut which repays close inspection. In the base of the wall outside the hut can be seen a semicircle of stones, the top of a water race, for this is the site of Birks Mill, a lead smelter which was working as early as 1699. Early in the next century it was producing about 60 tons of lead a year.

The path climbs obliquely up the side of Birks Fell which displays the usual layer cake geology of this part of the Dales. Limestone is replaced by the Yoredale beds which in turn are covered by the millstone grit of the summit and the stakes marking the early reaches of the track give way to cairns.

Where the steepness eases, a wall is met and this runs up on to the flat top of the ridge. The trig point (S5499) atop Firth Fell gives good views of Fountains Fell and the back of Penyghent.

The joy which comes from walking the tops is a sum of many little parts and on one bright October morning it was the delight of crunching over frosted peat which added much to the morning.

The Birks Fell ridge is accompanied by a wall and this can be followed north-westwards, passing a walled sheep creep, some shallow quarries near shallow but extensive Birks Tarn, and a small, roofless barn-like structure built in to the wall.The original summit is marked by a well-constructed cairn off to the right-hand side of the wall. The cairn is presumably of some antiquity: it surely predates the first survey of the district, for why else would a tiny 2,000-foot contour ring have appeared on the maps otherwise? The top is virtually flat!

A shepherd's cairn on the north-eastern slope, near the "summit", is a better place to sit down, for it gives a head-on view of the wooded, steep and deeply cut valley of Buckden Beck across Wharfedale.

The other side of the old road, from Litton, is a bit steeper than the Buckden approach and, on a wet day, could well have given problems to descending corpse bearers. They would have bolstered their spirits with the knowledge that the Queen's Arms, or more likely its predecessor, was at the foot of the fell. An evening stroll along the lower part of the track nowadays is likely to be accompanied by a host of scurrying rabbits.

In order to visit the "new" top of Birks Fell from the former "summit", it is necessary either to cross walls or to descend and re-ascend the ridge. There is no right-of-way along the top, though it is obvious that walkers do make the traverse of the ridge. Along one section, across rather wet and groughy ground, the wall is replaced by a wire fence.

The recently promoted top lies on the far side of the ridge wall near to the aptly named Sugar Loaf. This appears as a bright green pimple from a distance, in contrast to the rest of the fell, and the reason soon becomes clear for a patch of limestone, complete with shake holes, nettles and thistles, surfaces here. The top is not marked but lies in an area of tussock grass.

The path between Halton Gill and Yockenthwaite crosses the ridge half a mile or so north-west of this top. Although it is shown on the map as a bridleway from the north, strangely it is not marked as such from the other side. It crosses the ridge at Horse Head Gate and is a section of the pack-horse route between Settle and Hawes. It was a regular part of the beat of curates from Arncliffe when Hubberholme church had no resident minister. Rev. Miles Wilson reported, in 1743, that divine service was held every Sunday except in winter when it took place every fortnight "because it is with great danger and difficulty I pass over very high mountains and large drifts of snow to the chapel."

Horse Head, the summit north-west of the Gate, does not reach 2,000 feet but its trig point gives fine views of the distant Lakeland mountains and, closer at hand, that group of fells which to many epitomises the Yorkshire Dales.

12
Three Peaks and Neighbours

The names Smith and Wynne-Edwards do not ring through the walker's hall of fame as do Stephenson and Wainright, but they ought to be remembered, for these two teachers from Giggleswick School originated the Three Peaks Walk.

Thousands have followed their pioneering ways if not exactly their footsteps, as it took some years for the present route to evolve, and the walk has developed into a local industry based on the cafe at Horton in Ribblesdale. Here you can breakfast early before you start, clock out and, much later, clock back in again! Walkers completing the circuit in under twelve hours are awarded a certificate.

Horton is certainly the most popular starting point now, though Chapel-le-Dale and Ribblehead are other natural beginnings, lying as they do in the valleys between two of the three. Most walkers favour an anti-clockwise route which tackles the climbing in short, sharp bursts followed by generally long and gradual descents.

An easy stroll, probably in company, past the church at Horton and then up the lane by the school, on the far side of Horton Bridge, leads the walker to Brackenbottom and the foot of the lowest and smallest, but to many the best, of the Three Peaks.

Penyghent

Penyghent, 2,277 feet, throws up its southern end in two giant steps that are the mountain's chief feature when seen in profile from Horton or from Fountains Fell. The crags which form the risers of this truncated staircase are gloriously picked out by snow and by the low light of early morning or evening. A few mild spring days can show them to advantage in another way, for then the mountain saxifrage will flower and give a splash of purple to the white limestone crags.

In one way Penyghent flatters to deceive, for its summit is a broad affair while its curtain of crags deserves, and promises to anyone halfway up them, an airy pinnacle. Still, this would be paradisical and we need to leave something for heaven: the fell has enough to marvel at without the need for perfection!

The first part of the ascent, over limestone pasture, is as full of interest as ever and those not hurrying round the Three Peaks trail can do far worse than spend five minutes on their knees, examining carefully a small area of turf. The botanist will have fun trying to identify the different types of little, white flowers while the non-scientist will enjoy the variety of shade and tone and, further afield, the view across Ribblesdale towards Ingleborough.

It is as well to bear this vegetational medley in mind, for soon everything changes with the underlying rock and a peaty moor is crossed – a moor which has suffered badly due to its position halfway up Penyghent. Recent estimates put the number of visitors to the summit each year at over 50,000, including perhaps 15,000 who are on the Three Peaks round. If the total were averaged out, it would put one visitor on the top of the fell every ten minutes, day and night, all year round.

Penyghent as seen from above Langcliffe, near Settle. (Geoffrey N. Wright)

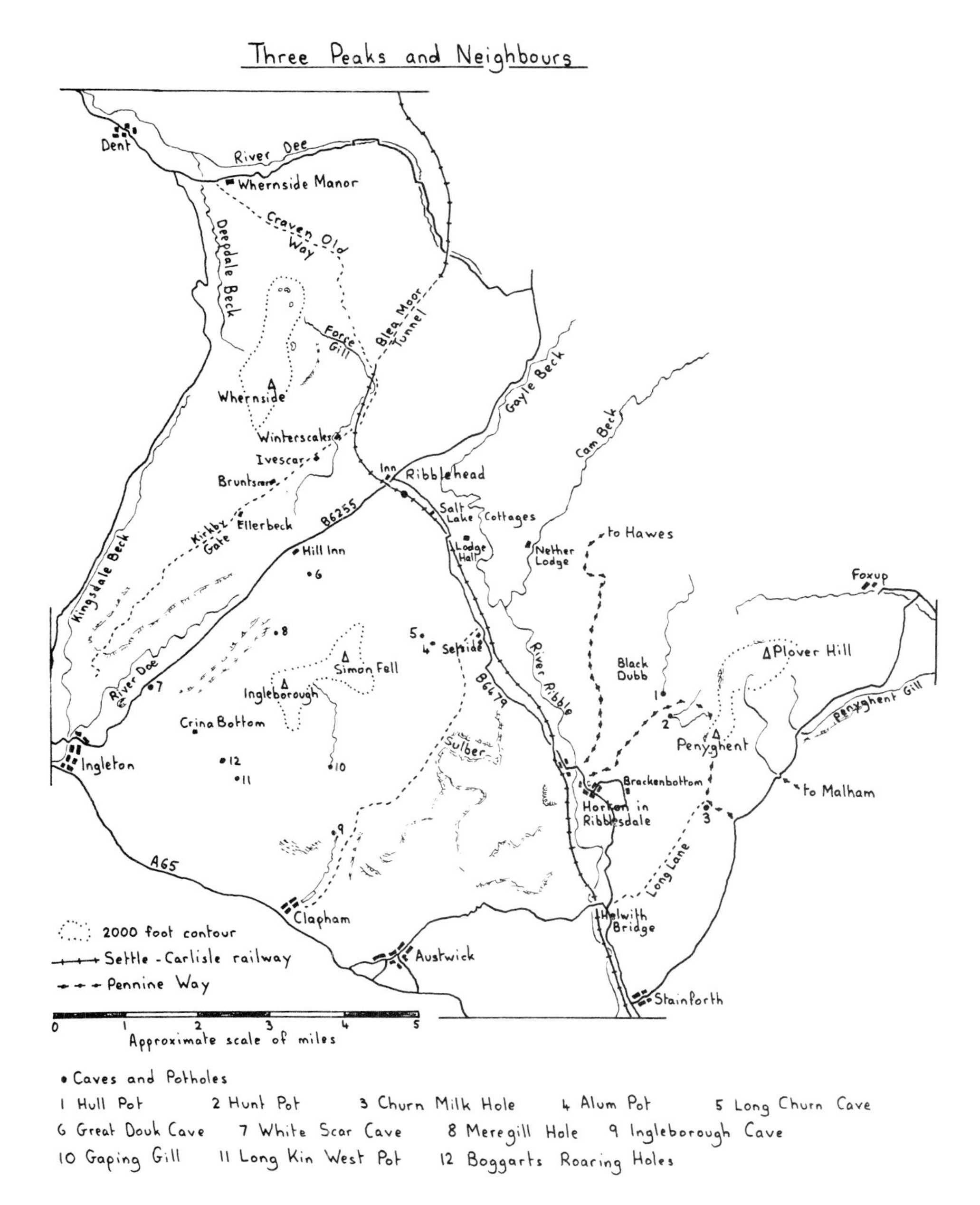

The fragile flora which develops on this wet, acid moorland is easily damaged and slow to regenerate. This, together with the soft nature of the underlying peat, led to the trampling of a broad, boggy swathe up the fellside as successive groups of visitors have walked ever wider to avoid the spreading morass. In the early 1980s, flights of wooden stairs and duckboard appeared on the section across the moor above Brackenbottom. Since then the problem has got worse and new solutions have been sought, culminating in the £500,000 Three Peaks Project which began in April 1987, following a comprehensive footpaths survey carried out the previous year.

This painted a very bleak picture of the state of paths on the Three Peaks, with over twelve out of the 40 miles of footpath in the area in a severely damaged state and another twelve needing immediate remedial work to avoid damage on a similar scale. On average, the "path" was over twelve yards wide while on the notorious Black Dubb Moss it was measured at over 150 yards across.

Various methods have been tried to rebuild the paths including a trumpeted "miracle cure" which involved the use of a chemical mixed in with the soil below the peat layer. This was supposed to harden the ground and turn it into a surface fit for walking on. At first things seemed to be going well on the stretch near Churn Milk Hole, south of Penyghent's summit, where it was first tried, and a hard path resulted which lasted through the summer and autumn of 1987. During the subsequent winter, though, the path was affected by regular freezing and thawing and by the end of January the entire length of the chemically hardened section, nearly 400 yards, had broken up into a sticky mess. The officers involved with the rebuilding of the paths now consider that a higher proportion of clay is necessary in the soil layer before the chemical method will work effectively.

The present attempts owe more to Blind Jack of Knaresborough than to modern science, though the work is being eased by the use of as much machinery as the fragile ground will hold.

The technique of floating paths across areas of wet ground was used by the famous Yorkshire road builder, and although the materials have changed, the methods remain pretty much the same. Today's path menders remove the peat and lay a layer of textile material on the subsoil, making the path back up to level with stone aggregate. In particularly wet areas, like the stretch beside the railway at Ribblehead below Whernside, a plastic grid, like chicken wire, is floated out over the peat and eight inches of stone laid on top. Here a dark Silurian stone from Horton is being used which blends in well with the gaunt arches of the viaduct and the peaty surroundings.

On Penyghent, all is not so compatible. The white, six-foot-wide streak of a path fairly glowed in the declining sunlight of a July evening in 1988, snaking upwards from the mini-building site with its quarter-scale dumper trucks and large pile of stone chippings at the top of the walled section of Pennine Way from Horton. It looked garish and unnatural, only slightly better than the duckboards above Brackenbottom, and hopefully, through usage, the path will eventually take on the subdued tones of its surroundings, for the lure of the area will not diminish and, although artificial paths take some of the joy out of walking, artificial sloughs take more.

Above the moor, on the ascent from Brackenbottom, Penyghent thrusts up its helm of crags, millstone grit above limestone, and the Pennine Way route is met at the wall which here marks the watershed. It is a fine climb up through the crags, followed by an anticlimactic stroll over grass, peat, and, at time of writing, a boardwalk, up to the summit which is marked by a large, untidy, sometimes litter-strewn cairn and a trig point carrying the benchmark S5776. The summit wall provides shelter on what would otherwise be a bleak top. The view is far-ranging, as is to be expected from such a central fell, and many of the hills described in this volume can be seen. The summit also gives intimate nearer views, such as the sinuous course of Penyghent Gill running down to the wooded slopes of Littondale, and leaves the Three Peaks walker in no doubt about the size of the task ahead.

The only blot on the landscape is Horton Quarry and its blue lagoon, a winter sight which never fails to remind this writer of Bishop Hever's nineteenth-century missionary hymn, substituting Yorkshire for Greenland's icy mountains, but retaining the punch-line "where every prospect pleases, And only man is vile".

Of the five rights-of-way leading to the summit, three are very heavily used, the two legs of the Pennine Way from Horton and from Dale Head, and the route from Brackenbottom. The Horton path is the descent for most Wayfarers, the recently rebuilt section giving way to a stony, walled track, Horton Scar Lane, for the last couple of gentle miles down to the village. The lane probably started as a monastic road, for the brothers of Fountains Abbey owned land in Horton.

Short diversions from the Pennine Way will bring the visitor to two contrasting potholes. At Hunt Pot a small stream plunges down a narrow vertical shaft in two leaps of 100 feet – the secret limestone underworld at its most secretive. Less than half a mile away Hull Pot displays itself for all the world to see, a great hole in the hillside, 100 yards long and 25 wide. In wet weather Hull Pot Beck cascades 50 feet to soak into a jumble of boulders on the floor and occasionally, after a really wet spell, the whole lot fills up and overflows.

One Pennine Wayfarer who certainly didn't have time for even short diversions was Michael Hartley, an MEB meter reader from Rugeley, who ran the Way over a very hot and dry weekend in July 1989 and broke the record by 4½ hours. His 2 days, 17 hours and 20 minutes for the 270-mile route can only be gasped at by the scores who toil up Penyghent's scarp on their way between Malham and Horton, an easy Way day, each year. The literally blistering run – Mr. Hartley was wearing a size eight shoe on his left foot and a size ten on his right by the end – was completed at an average speed of just over four miles an hour. His longest stop, during a long weekend which began in Kirk Yetholm at 3am on Friday, was for nineteen minutes, and Mr. Hartley lost ten pounds in weight and ran his way through 27 pairs of socks and five sets of shoes.

The approach from Dale Head passes by the large collapsed swallet of Churn Milk Hole and crosses some wet ground by means of a well-built path before climbing up by the wall through the crags. It was while descending by this route recently that the whole purpose of the Three Peaks Project came to me. They are going to build a narrow gauge railway round the lot of them and the track bed is being temporarily disguised as rebuilt footpaths! A quieter way of reaching Churn Milk Hole is by way of Long Lane, a track which climbs gently from Helwith Bridge and which gives the purest approach to Penyghent from the south.

For the walker who wishes to shun crowds, the alternatives are early morning, evening, midweek or even, at the busy times, an approach from Foxup. This is not the most exciting way of climbing the fell, rather a stealthy sneak up from the back, along a path which has only recently been shown as a right-of-way, but it does give the advantage of high season solitude, and on a day when Penyghent is crawling with walkers or runners or cyclists, the lone pedestrian might be tempted to curtail his travels on Penyghent's little-known neighbour.

Looking towards Penyghent from Runscar, above Ribblehead. (Geoffrey N. Wright)

Penyghent, viewed from limestone clints west of Malham Tarn. (Tom Richardson).

Plover Hill

Plover Hill, 2,231 feet, shares with Simon Fell on Ingleborough the status of subsidiary summit to one of Yorkshire's most famous mountains. Although it possesses a fine line of crags along its western side, one of the most well-constructed and tallest dry stone walls in England across the length of its top, and a much larger area above 2,000 feet, Plover Hill has few devotees when compared with its 46-foot higher neighbour. If Penyghent has been likened to a crouching lion, then Plover Hill has more the profile of a sleeping hippo.

The hill is, of course, named after those aerial acrobats the plovers, two of which are often seen and heard on these heights. The golden plover, with its plaintive call and pointed wings, and the lapwing, its drawn-out *peewit* echoing in sound the mood of the fells, are often companions on the tops.

The western edge of the fell, known as Penyghent Side, displays a fine band of crags topped with some huge perched blocks, but apart from this and a few rashes of boulders on the higher slopes, all is grass. The top, a rather dull plateau, is crossed by several walls and four of these meet near the summit.

One of them, of high and solid construction, follows the watershed down from Penyghent and has a distinct path along much of its western side. A stile over the cross-wall shows the path's elevation to right-of-way status. There was neither path nor stile ten years ago. At the Plover Hill end there is now a signpost pointing the way down to the Foxup road path. About halfway between the two tops is a small patch of bouncing bog.

The summit is large and flat with a cairn at its eastern end overlooking Littondale's bright green fields and darker patches of woodland. Penyghent is not seen to best advantage from here, its crags being obscured by its bulk, but Fountains and Darnbrook fells rise boldly across the valley of Penyghent Gill.

A round trip, from Horton to Penyghent and then on to Plover Hill, returning along the path across Foxup Moor, makes a good evening walk especially in the brightness after a shower. There is plenty to attract the eye, particularly on the descent from Plover Hill. A line of shake holes marches ruler-straight over Blaydike Moss across the sparkling wet Foxup Moor. The head of deeply trenched Littondale darkens in the approaching dusk. Perched blocks stand hugely on the crags of Penyghent Side and, glowering large and square in the west, dark in silhouette, rises the massive table top of Ingleborough. In the brighter light of morning there is an unusual oblique view of the arches of Ribblehead Viaduct with Whernside looming behind.

A longer round, from Foxup, can take in Fountains Fell and Darnbrook Fell as well.

This section started by describing the beginning of the Three Peaks round and the wall corner below Penyghent Side where the Foxup Moor path starts its descent towards Hull Pot is as good a place as any to rejoin it. A descent to Hull Pot Beck is followed by a climb to the worst bit of the whole walk, Black Dubb Moss. A quaking bog which offers no mercy to the previously dry-footed, it can be avoided only by a long detour round the enclosure which it lies in. Following one particularly gruesome crossing of Black Dubb, I determined to fight back, and on the next round, with my brother, I brought two bin liners each. The theory was that we pulled these up over our boots and legs and waded through the mire. The practice was that we both fell over after the first, faltering footsteps, much to the delight of a party of 30 who had gathered to watch our experiment.

The next mile is better, undulating over an area of drumlins to cross the

Pennine Way as it starts its climb to Cam End. Then follows a lovely walk across limestone pastures, over the natural span of God's Bridge and down to Nether Lodge. A farm track is joined here and all is plain sailing, crossing the young Ribble by a bridge to Lodge Hall and its clear, cold water. The track rises to the road which is followed past the railway terrace of Salt Lake cottages, on the site of a shanty town, to Ribblehead where the route reaches the territory of the second peak.

Whernside

Whernside, 2,415 feet, is the highest of the three and, rising starkly from the moor at Ribblehead, it dominates the heads of Ribblesdale and that of the Doe. Here the Settle-Carlisle line, curving round towards Blea Moor on the massive 24-arch viaduct, is cut down to size. From nearly 1,500 feet higher, it looks like a model.

Since 1974 Whernside has been the highest fell in planners' Yorkshire (and if the present boundary is taken to be the wall along the top then, horror of horrors, the trig point is actually in Cumbria), but it has always been the summit of the West Riding and is overtopped in the real county only by Mickle Fell.

The configuration of its rocks has resulted in a less dramatic outline than that presented by Penyghent and Ingleborough, and so Whernside has to rely on sheer height and bulk in order to attract the eye in views from a distance.

It is a pity that Whernside is know to many only as a result of its place on the Three Peaks round, for the usual route up the fell was a ghastly thrutch up a sloppy slope above Winterscales Farm. The first time I walked round the Three Peaks there was a wall at the top of the climb but, ten years later in the mid-eighties this had largely disappeared, being replaced by an ugly, stony scar. Recently, and rightly, the use of this route, which was never a right-of-way, has been discouraged and a more natural line, following the Craven Way alongside the railway from Winterscales before turning to tackle the north end of Whernside, has been promoted and given right-of-way status.

The old way up did serve one purpose, in my mind at least, for, as geologists have their Richter Scale to measure the force of earthquakes, I have long used a "Whernside Scale" for ascents. On this gauge, the climb up from Winterscales merited seven out of ten. Ten is vertical.

Whernside looks at its glowering best on a day when a wild wind is rattling up the dale and the cloud hangs low over the summit. In the days of steam, and today when a special is running, a trail of white exhaust being blown down off the viaduct and swirling round the arches at Ribblehead, added further to the atmosphere of the scene.

This remote spot must have seemed like the end of the earth to the Midland Railway surveyors who tramped out the route of the line. John Sharland, a Tasmanian who was one of the pioneers, found himself snowed up for three weeks at Gearstones, then an inn on the Ingleton-Hawes turnpike. The navvies who built the railway, living in a settlement of 2,000 souls at Batty Green hard by the viaduct, some of whom had worked the world over, certainly agreed that this was "one of the wildest, windiest, coldest and dreariest localities" anywhere. Those who stuck it out lived here for seven years while the viaduct and Bleamoor Tunnel were constructed.

The path from the road to Winterscales passes beneath the viaduct, giving ample opportunity to study this, the biggest single piece of building on the line. Each of its two dozen arches has a span of 45 feet and the foundations for the pillars had to go down 25 feet through peat and clay to find solid rock. At its highest point, the tallest pillar is 165 feet from foundations to track level. Every sixth pier is extra strong while all are made of huge stones. Some of them weigh seven or eight tons with the courses being over a yard thick. The arches are turned in brick and about 1½ million were used. A brick-making machine stood near the viaduct and could produce 20,000 a day.

There were days when it was too windy for men to work for fear of being blown off the structure. An apocryphal tale tells of a man's hat being blown off his head, under an arch and on to his head again. A no doubt later version tells of a navvy who followed the same route! Trains have been forced to a standstill on the viaduct by the force of the wind.

Over a century of such weather has got into the viaduct's joints. Many of the pillars have carried a lattice of scaffolding. They bear a sign (in German and French as well as English) to beware falling masonry and the rails have been reduced to single track. After many years of neglect the authorities will now have to put in the proper level of investment to bring this great work back to standard. What an insult to the memory of the men who had the flair and imagination to design it and those who had the muscles and guts to built it, if the viaduct at Batty Moss had been left to deteriorate as an excuse to shut the line and the track downgraded to a walkers' or cyclists' route as one proposition stated!

Walking beside the tracks, the former railway cottages at Bleamoor Sidings are passed and the moor opens out. The railway drops into the cutting leading to the southern mouth of Bleamoor Tunnel and the path crosses a bridge next to an aqueduct carrying Force Gill. This stream, rising high on Whernside's north-eastern slopes below Mill Stone Brow, caused the railway engineers a great deal of trouble, washing away temporary bridges and inundating quarries, before it was channelled. The stones of the aqueduct were set in hot asphalt to make sure it stayed waterproof.

There is a good view of the tunnel mouth from the bridge and the spoil tips from the shafts show its underground route, curling away to the north-east. There were originally seven shafts which, together with the two mouths, meant sixteen working faces while the nearly 1½-mile-long tunnel was under construction. It still took four years to dig under Blea Moor and because the tunnel intersected different strata it had to be brick lined throughout.

The path to Whernside follows the Craven Way track for a while longer before turning off to climb to Whernside's north ridge. Force Gill has two fine waterfalls which are worth visiting and a diversion may also be made to Greensett Tarn lying in a wet hollow above a limestone area. This is one of several tarns on the fell's northern slopes, the others, Whernside Tarns, lying half a mile or so further north, across the wall. All these tarns are alive with gulls which wheel and screech in a most seaside-like manner. Once on the ridge, the wall can be followed south to the trig point.

Whernside is a long whaleback of a mountain and a long, gentle and satisfying walk can be made of an ascent by the south-west ridge from Ingleton. Two thousand feet of altitude is gained over about seven miles, a definite two on the Whernside Scale!

Oddies Lane, the other end of the Roman Road already met on Drumaldrace and Dodd Fell, can be followed as far as the footpath between Beezleys and Twistleton Hall at the foot of Twistleton Scar End. Here a fine path zigzags its way up the steep slope into an area of limestone around Ewes Top which is marked by a large cairn. The path up Twistleton Scar End can also be reached

Whernside from near Ribblehead – a typical scene in the heart of the Three Peaks country. (Geoffrey N. Wright)

Dentdale, as seen from the cairn near the tarns on Whernside. (Geoffrey N. Wright)

Ribblehead viaduct and, beyond, the flanks of Whernside. (Derek G. Widdicombe)

by way of the western branch of the Ingleton Waterfalls Walk though it is necessary to pay a fee to follow this route. Few would begrudge paying to be in the delightful and, in wet weather, awe-inspiring surroundings of Pecca Falls and Thornton Force, but the walk round the glens is grand enough to spend a good half-day on and it seems a shame to miss some of the detail through rushing to get to Whernside. Use Oddies Lane and save your money, and the Waterfalls Walk, for a wet Sunday afternoon.

Once past Ewes Top all is plain sailing in the company of the ridge wall and the main excitement comes from looking across the dale to the ever-changing profile of Ingleborough. The underlying rock strata is reflected in the wall which changes from limestone to millstone grit on Rigg End.

An alternative descent, and one which would add a couple of extra miles to the day, is to descend to Winterscales by the Force Gill route already described and then follow the Craven Way as it joins up the series of farms – Ivescar, Bruntscar, Ellerbeck – huddled below Whernside's southern flank. From Ellerbeck the Way, known here as Kirkby Gate, climbs slowly over Scales Moor back to Ewes Top.

The northern end of the Craven Way climbs up above Whernside Manor, now a caving centre, and along Wold End it is a walled lane. From the end of the walled section, at Boot of the Wold, the northern slopes of Whernside can be tackled directly. There are a couple of fine cairns and a shelter where the slope eases just below Whernside Tarns and then the summit wall is reached on Knoutberry Hill.

The easiest ascent of Whernside is the dull mile or so plod up over Cable Rake from the top of the Kingsdale road. A wall is followed for over half the way and then it's over to the nose. This route has one advantage over all the others apart, from its shortness. On a bright winter's morning nothing on the trudge can prepare you for the wonderland which appears on looking over the summit wall. We came this way one winter when the top stretch of the road was blocked by drifts and the snow was covering all bar the capstones of the wall. A white wonderland stretched out to the south with Ingleborough and Penyghent rising up like a pair of great, beached Moby Dicks with the sinuous black thread of the railway line snaking between them.

The trig point stands by a little kink in the wall and on its northern side. It carries benchmark 2982 and is generally a fairly busy place. The view is good, as it should be from the highest place in the West Riding of Yorkshire. Ingleborough is seen as the highest of three great steps and looks particularly big to the Three Peaks walker who is eating his butties and studying his map. Penyghent seems but a memory and looks far enough away to be just that. If Lancastrians are allowed a mention in this work, then they will be gratified at the sight of Pendle Hill through the dip between Ingleborough and Simon Fell. Looking over the wall, Gragareth and Great Coum lounge across Kingsdale, Baugh Fell and the Howgills lead the eye on to Lakeland and the imagination follows the railway under Blea Moor to emerge on Great Knoutberry Hill with the Mallerstang fells beyond.

For the Three Peaks walker, there is only one way down and that follows the wall south for half a mile before peeling off to the valley after a steep and rocky section. This has always been a fast descent but the last time I did it, straining to catch the Hill Inn before Sunday afternoon closing time, records for running downstairs were probably broken. The steps have had even more of a hammering since then. At the bottom, by Bruntscar, limestone is regained and there is no need for artificiality. The walk down the lane to Chapel-le-Dale always seems longer on the ground than it looks on the map but time can be profitably spent in wondering whether you really did see a wonderful collection of old agricultural vehicles through the window of a large, modern barn at Bruntscar.

It is axiomatic that whatever time you walk into the Hill Inn it will be crowded. Refrain from shouting "Out of my way, you car-borne wastrels, it is my right to stand first at this bar, for I have walked fifteen hard miles to get here", for half of them will ignore you and the other half will chorus "So have we!"

The Three Peaks walker, aided by a half-hour's rest and what that inveterate nineteenth-century pedestrian George Borrow described as 'a jug of good ale', will leave the Hill Inn refreshed and hopefully in the right direction to tackle Ingleborough. Readers of this work must leave that culminating Yorkshire glory for a while longer: Ingleborough has a supporter.

Simon Fell

Simon Fell, 2,133 feet, is a subsidiary top on the broad ridge which runs from Ingleborough towards Ribblehead. The summit lies less than a mile north-east of the top of Ingleborough, but I doubt whether it is visited by one in a hundred of those who yearly reach the trig point.

From Ribblehead there is a rise of nearly 800 feet to the top of Park Fell and then, after a slight depression, a walk along the edge of the escarpment to where a wall is crossed by a stile. This wall can then be followed to the ridge wall which bends and twists to the summit. This stands just north of the wall and is marked by a few pieces of stone and wood. In 1971, Nick Wright *(English Mountain Summits)* commented that the wall was in good condition and implored visitors to take care to avoid damaging it. It's still sound throughout its length on the Ingleborough side although starting to buckle a bit by the summit and now has a topping of barbed wire.

This route, over Park Fell from the road to Colt Park, is straightforward and is an easy way to the top. A shorter but steeper ascent can be made from the Hill Inn at Chapel-le-Dale, following the well-worn track for Ingleborough before doubling back at the top of the steep climb from Humphrey Bottom. Both of these routes have the advantage of landing the walker on the right side of the wall for the meagre cairn.

The other way to get to the top is to follow another well-worn track to Ingleborough from Horton in Ribblesdale. Simon Fell dominates the early stages of the walk, especially the section around Sulber Nick, and many walkers must have thought the lower fell to be Ingleborough itself, only to find the latter looming up beyond. The path can be deserted on Simon Fell Breast and the slope to the summit plateau tackled directly, or it can be followed to the wall on the col between the two fells. The second option, though a bit longer, at least enables the walker to get on the right side of the wall for the cairn.

Ingleborough dominates the view from the top, though it is a bulkier Ingleborough than that seen from most directions. On a wintry morning, with the snow lying in drifts alongside the sinuous wall and with sunshine picking out scree and scar, it is a grand sight.

Like all the neighbouring hills, Simon Fell's base is of carboniferous limestone which here exhibits all the attributes associated with this wonderful rock. Of the many features in the hill's cellars, three are particularly noteworthy and two can be explored with care, while the other is grand enough to make a view from outside good enough.

Alum Pot, formerly Hell Pot, a much better descriptive name, lies on the east side of the fell, above the hamlet of Selside. I have on my desk a pewter half-pint tankard with the inscription "Plough Inn, Selside" scratched on the bottom. No doubt 'borrowed' by a Victorian ancestor during a railway excursion from the mill town to Ribblesdale, it is a tangible link with time and place. There is neither a Plough Inn at Selside now nor a Red Lion. Perhaps they had already closed by when that inveterate explorer of the Dales, Harry Speight, passed through towards the end of the last century. He found the place half deserted.

After paying a small fee at Selside Farm, Alum Pot can be reached up a lane, walled at first, which leaves the road at a bend just north of the hamlet. From where this track turns to the south (it was the old road to Clapham), a clump of trees can be seen on the fellside. This indicates the location of the pot, a great hole, oval in shape and 130 feet along its long axis, which is 200 feet down to the bottom. In wet weather a small beck tumbles down its southern side, turning into a curtain of spray as it falls.

If Alum Pot is a classic and very well-developed vertical pothole and manifestly for experts only, then nearby Long Churn Cave provides a horizontal contrast and it has long been used to give would-be cavers a taste of the underground. It is safe to enter Upper Long Churn in dry weather and follow the stream passage for a couple of hundred yards. Take a good torch and expect to get wet feet, a small price, together with the fee payable at Selside Farm on whose land the cave lies, for a superb introduction to a fine sport.

Around on the northern side of Simon Fell, the area above the Hill Inn also repays time spent in exploration, for there are large areas of limestone pavement and the third noteworthy cave and another which may be explored. Though not as easy to enter as Long Churn – Great Douk Cave is defended by a six-foot waterfall – once inside a 100-yard length of the stream passage can be safely explored. It passes through a couple of chambers on its way to the bottom of Little Douk Pot where daylight can be seen above.

Although there is plenty of interest to detain the walker on Simon Fell, it is more than likely that steps will be hurried in order to reach the real target of most visitors to this triangle of high ground between Ribblehead, Ingleton and Settle.

Ingleborough

Ingleborough, 2,372 feet, is the Yorkshire fell *par excellence*. It is visited by more people than any other and scores toil up its rocky flanks who have never heard of Mickle Fell, let alone Yockenthwaite Moor. Its pre-eminence lies not in absolute altitude, for neighbouring Whernside as well as Mickle Fell overtop it, but rather because of form and position. The configuration of its rocks have given Ingleborough an unmistakeable profile while its location, standing slightly aloof from the mass of the Yorkshire Pennines and surrounded by deep valleys, makes it the centre of attention in many views, from main roads as well as hilltops.

Ingleborough tells the geological story of all the fells mentioned in this work, with the exception of the Howgills, and how graphically and visibly it depicts its history! Stand at the foot of Kingsdale in the vicinity of the lane to Twistleton Hall and age after age of earth-building and destruction can be read in the chapters of rocks. The effects of the different strata on the present-day landscape stand out clearly for the mountain's flat top, stepped sides, horizontal scars and the wide valley from which it rises are all manifestations of the stuff it is made from.

There, across Kingsdale are the quarries of Skirwith and Storrs Common, opened for the extraction of tough roadstone from the anciently tilted, folded and then planed-off pre-Cambrian grits and slates of the basement beds. On to this ground-down surface were deposited in turn the rocks of the Carboniferous era.

The Great Scar Limestone demonstrates its pureness (it is 98 per cent calcium carbonate) over on White Scars where a show cave enables the visitor to see it from the inside. Deposited in a shallow sea and composed of the bones and shells of marine creatures, the limestone has few fossils large enough to see. It is not porous but has a well-developed system of vertical joints and horizontal bedding planes which are attacked by water, giving rise to the limestone pavements, potholes, caves, scars, dry valleys and gorges which are such a feature of the mountain.

After the limestone was laid down, a large river delta encroached on the shallow sea from the north-east and the Yoredale rocks were laid down in water which was alternately clear or muddy, sometimes with shifting sandbanks and wandering channels. The repetition of these fluctuations has given rise to the repeated pattern of rocks and the stepped form of Ingleborough and Penyghent and of Whernside and Wensleydale.

Later, when delta conditions became firmly established, the millstone grit was laid down. Thin coal seams in the rock mark the beginnings of tropical swamp conditions which prevailed when the area was much further south. The coal measures have been eroded from what is now the top of Ingleborough but they were mined at Ingleton until 1937. How can the same kind of rock as that once found on the top of the mountains occur hundreds of feet underground just five miles away? A great series of faults rent the area throwing the rocks on which Ingleton now stands over a mile below those of the mountain top. When miners worked the deepest seams of the Ingleton coalfield, they were still hundreds of feet above the rocks which at present form the top of Ingleborough.

Since the rocks were first deposited, millions of years of erosion have taken place, gradually lowering the whole of the Pennines while valleys have been carved out, cutting into what was once a plateau and separating the different fells from each other. The ice ages contributed to the landscape, deepening and widening valleys and freezing the ground so that rivers ran on the surface rather than through the limestone. Ice sheets and glaciers scoured the surface, carting away soil from the uplands and plastering it on the lowlands, carrying boulders from place to place and leaving them stranded as erratics. On to this landscape, swept clean by ice, developed the vegetation which would have been seen by the first Mesolithic settlers who arrived about halfway between the ice ages and us.

The fell tops were maybe much like they are today, covered in heather and peat and with wet areas of cotton-grass and moss. The fellsides below would have had a covering of open woodland, rather as can be seen of the sides of a few dales today, with oak and birch predominating while the lower slopes were of dense oak forest floored with thick undergrowth. The valley floors would have been avoided altogether, for they were covered with unpassable swamp overhung by thick clumps of willow and alder.

Possibly the early settlers stood on Ingleborough and gazed across tree-girt valleys to Whernside and Penyghent. Certainly people have been visiting the summit for hundreds, if not thousands, of years for there is tangible proof as well as the evidence of imagination to suggest that early folk looked on Ingleborough as something special. It has been a beacon hill, it was fortified by people who built circular huts on its summit, it has acted as the local racecourse and for a very brief time indeed it possessed a castellated round tower.

Ingleborough was a must for early tourists, travellers of the Romantic age who certainly romanticised about its height: it was thought to be 5,280 feet high by one and 3,987 feet by another. It may possibly feel as high as this to the Three Peaks walker approaching from the direction of the Hill Inn at Chapel-le-Dale, or if rather more Old Peculier than ought to be has been consumed, the walker may well feel a mile high.

I once came this way with a regular Three Peaks companion who fitted the last description well. This was a November round and so less time than usual had been spent imbibing in view of the limited hours of daylight. Crossing the beautiful short-cropped turf and limestone pavements around Southerscales he was heard to comment, mostly to himself: "I didn't realise it was so good round here, I don't remember walking this stretch before." A lot of money has been spent on path improvements along this section, another part of the Three Peaks Project.

The rest of the way, especially the steep climb up from Humphrey Bottom, can prove the hardest bit of the whole walk, but once on the col things are easier. The walk up to the summit plateau across angular gritstone boulders raises the sense of anticipation and then the great top opens out, a gently tilted cap, half a mile round.

The sixteen-acre plateau was defended by a stone wall probably dating from the Iron Age and built by the Brigantes, a northern tribe which the Romans found a tough nut to crack. The wall was likely never completed for some parts of the plateau edge are steep enough not to need an artificial defence. In places above the northern and eastern slopes it is fourteen feet thick and it may have been up to twelve feet high. We can view the wall as a last redoubt of the Brigantes against the Roman conquerors or maybe as a first-century status symbol for a local chief. Whatever its origin, a lot of work went in to its construction. Inside the wall are a number of circular stone hut bases around 30 feet in diameter which may have been home to defenders or pastoralists.

A pile of stones at the western end of the plateau marks the site of a shelter, a round tower constructed in 1830 at the height of the Romantic tourist boom, but which was fated to be partially destroyed by inebriated revellers after the opening ceremony got out of hand! Nowadays they might well be looked on as conservationists rather than vandals. Time and generations of subsequent visitors have completed the slighting but a few curved stones are still visible.

Our own century has seen the construction of an Ordnance Survey triangulation pillar carrying benchmark plaque S5619 and a cross-wall shelter with a view indicator built in the centre. The Ingleton Fell Rescue Team built this in 1953 to commemorate the coronation of the queen.

The view is good and far-ranging though it would be better were the top not so flat. It is a view of contrasts. To the west a late afternoon sun sparkles on Morecambe Bay and highlights some of the Lakeland giants including Helvellyn, Skiddaw and Coniston Old Man. Northwards and eastwards roll the fells of Yorkshire, green and dun, from the whaleback of Whernside across the Greta valley all the way round to distant Great Whernside above Nidderdale. Most of the fells described in this work can be seen from the top of Ingleborough and an interesting and satisfying twenty minutes can be spent trying to place as many as possible. South-west, over the widening Ribble Valley, rises Pendle Hill, one beacon hill seen from another. It is easy to imagine the speed at which an alarm could be spread by using this simple system, on a clear day or night at least, but pity the poor folk who carried the fuel up. On Queen Victoria's golden jubilee, in June 1887, a massive bonfire blazed on Ingleborough, one of a chain which

Ingleborough from Beezley Farm near Ingleton. (Christine Whitehead)

also included Pendle as well as Blencathra and Skiddaw. Twelve tons of material were consumed and the beacon was visible from near Leeds. Spectators on the summit counted nearly 60 other blazes.

Walkers usually look forward to eating their butties on a summit but this is not to be recommended on Ingleborough for it is occupied by a particularly predatory family of sheep who come and outstare and hypnotise the visitor in to feeding them. This must be the prime heaf for ovine Yorkshire yuppies.

The summit always attracts a sprinkling of visitors but the last Sunday in April guarantees a crowd. It is the occasion of the annual Three Peaks Race, a highlight in the fell runner's diary since it was first run in 1954. The route varies only slightly from the usual pedestrian round but the times involved can only make the plodding pedestrian stagger. The record for this 22-mile round involving a total ascent of over 4,500 feet stands at just over 2½ hours. The race starts and finishes on Horton in Ribblesdale playing field which is turned into a car park for the day and the mass start sends the runners off on an exciting charge to the bridge over the Ribble before they disappear up the Pennine Way track towards Penyghent. Such is the popularity of the race that the men's field has to be restricted to 500. In 1986, 345 of the runners had entered the race before, 139 of them were veterans (over 40) and 25 of the entrants were aged over 50. A sure sign that some people never learn, even with age!

My brother entered for the first time a couple of years ago, and so myself and nephew John were stationed at the top of the slope leading up from the Simon Fell col, a good vantage point, for most of the route from the Hill Inn can be seen. This is also the last climb for weary limbs, coming at about the 17-mile mark and the field is well spread out. The col holds a cluster of tents for medical facilities, Raynet operators and marshalls. Peter came grimacing up the rocky path, John held out the bottle of glucose drink for his dad, and the fellow in front grabbed it! We managed to retrieve it with good grace before it had all gone and poured it down its rightful recipient who went on to complete the race in a very commendable time.

The descent route for runners is that followed by many who climb Ingleborough, coming up from Horton and tackling the ascent gradually over a distance of nearly six miles. The path's interest is concentrated in its middle reaches, where it crosses the limestone of Sulber, and the final approach to the summit. The section along Simon Fell Breast is a rather tedious walk across a peaty fellside striped by drainage ditches.

The most popular way of climbing Ingleborough, a seven-mile round trip from the car park, is from Ingleton. It is a straightforward walk with the objective in view for most of the way. Halfway up is the isolated farm of Crina Bottom in its well-sheltered hollow where we nearly abandoned our plans for the summit one February Sunday afternoon in order to go poly-bag sledging down one of the gullies. The well-trodden path goes straight-up, climbing a steep, peaty moor before reaching the short and sharp rocky steps up on to the summit. A more circuitous route, leaving the path at the stile over the intake wall and meandering across the limestone pavements of White Scars to Meregill Hole before picking up the path from the Hill Inn at Humphrey Bottom, might put the day's mileage into double figures, but it will more than double the pleasure.

The royal road to Ingleborough, though, is undoubtedly the one from Clapham. For sustained interest and variety there are few approaches to any mountain in Britain to touch it. The surprising thing is, with so much to catch the eye and hold the attention on the ascent, that anybody ever reaches the summit.

The formidable bulk of Ingleborough towers over Chapel-le-Dale. (G.V. Berry)

Ingleborough from the north Greta valley showing the point where the river goes underground.

It is possible to ignore the charms of Clapham itself, difficult because of its juxtaposition of stream, bridge and buildings and its air of being a much-loved and looked-after place, but just possible. It is possible to disregard the delights of the walk along Clapdale Drive by taking the track to Clapdale Farm. In doing so, the walker will save the small fee payable in order to walk through the grounds of Ingleborough Hall but will miss one of the finest valleys in Yorkshire. It is the result of landscape improvements made by the Farrer family over several generations. The lake was dammed in 1833, both to make a feature and to provide a reliable water supply for the village. Around the lake the woods are particularly beautiful, containing many fine specimen trees some of which were introduced by the most famous of the Farrers, the botanist, Reginald. A nature trail through the estate has been named after him. He worked mostly in the Far East and the observant will spot some of the bamboo he introduced here.

It is possible to walk past Ingleborough Cave with its entrance at the foot of a mighty limestone scar without visiting the subterranean wonders it holds. The quarter-mile stretch open to visitors contains some of the finest stalagmite and stalactite formations in the country with descriptive names like the Elephant's Legs, the Pillar and Skittle Alley.

It is, I suppose, just possible to keep your head down and avert your eyes from the 100-foot-high walls of the narrow and precipitous Trow Gill, a gorge carved out by an ancient stream and now decked with conifers and with many species of mosses and lichens, ferns and shrubs. The gorge contracts from a width of a hundred feet at its entrance to eight at its steep northern exit.

It is absolutely impossible to ignore, disregard, walk past or avert the eyes from the next feature, reached after half a mile of at first dry valley and then open fellside. Gaping Gill is so vastly and obviously dangerous, a 360-foot gullet, eight feet wide and twenty long at the top, which lies in a wide grassy funnel. It swallows Fell Beck at one gulp, sending it spraying and clouding down, the highest waterfall in Britain, to be swallowed up in the vast gloomy hall of the Main Chamber. Large enough to hold York Minster, it was not a Yorkshireman who first entered this immense crypt, but an intrepid French cave explorer, Edouard Alfred Martel, whose descent on August 1, 1895 opened a chapter of exploration still being continued today in the far-reaching ramifications of Ingleborough's underground.

The most important event to happen since that first downward climb into the unknown occurred when cavers completed the connection between Gaping Gill and Ingleborough Cave. Tests involving dropping four hundredweight of ammonium sulphate and later a ton of salt down Gaping Gill were carried out as far back as 1900, and proved that water indeed flowed between the two. These trials indicated that it took between a week and a fortnight for the water to flow between engulfment and resurgence. It took generations of cavers the best part of a century to force a way through a series of caves undreamed of by the early explorers to make a human link. Slowly and gradually places with names like Whitsun Series, Far Country, Clay Cavern and Radagast's Revenge gave up their secrets and on May 28, 1983, the underground link was finally made.

Ingleborough's massive limestone plinth is riddled with many more potholes and caves, especially in the area south and west of Newby Moss where can be found the 350-foot-deep Long Kin West Pot and the Boggarts Roaring Holes, so named because of a former local pastime of trundling stones down it to disturb the occupant who, of course, roared out his disapproval.

The Clapham path to the summit follows Fell Beck for a hundred yards or so from Gaping Gill before turning north-west to aim for the top of Little

Ingleborough, the fell's dumpy southern ridge. The summit is less than half a mile away, an easy walk giving the visitor time to think about all the marvels seen on the way up.

Clear weather is all that is required to turn this into a truly unforgettable day, one of many which will be experienced by the walker who spends some time exploring Yorkshire's high hills.

TABLE 1. Yorkshire Summits above 2,000 feet.

Arranged in order of Altitude.

The name is that most commonly used when more than one is found on the map.

Heights are in feet.

Name	Height	Grid Ref.	1:50000	1:25000
Mickle Fell	2,585	NY 804243	91	31
Whernside	2,415	SD 738814	98	2
Ingleborough	2,372	SD 741745	98	2
Great Shunner Fell	2,349	SD 848972	98	30
High Seat	2,326	NY 802012	91/92	
Great Whernside	2,310	SE 002739	98	30
Buckden Pike	2,303	SD 960787	98	30
Archy Styrigg	2,280	NY 802003	91/92	
Penyghent	2,277	SD 838733	98	2
Hugh Seat	2,260	SD 808991	98	
Great Coum	2,254	SD 700835	98	2
Long Crag	2,250	NY 842252	91	31
Plover Hill	2,231	SD 848752	98	2/30
Baugh Fell	2,224	SD 742916	98	
The Calf	2,218	SD 668965	98	
Lovely Seat	2,215	SD 879950	98	30
Calders	2,211	SD 670960	98	
Bram Rigg Top	2,205	SD 668965	98	
Great Knoutberry Hill	2,205	SD 788871	98	2
Rogan's Seat	2,205	NY 919030	91/92	30
Fountains Fell	2,192	SD 864715	98	2/10
Dodd Fell	2,192	SD 840845	98	2/30
Water Crag	2,192	NY 928046	91/92	30
Sails	2,185	SD 808965	98	
White Mossy Hill	2,150	NY 828025	91/92	
Simon Fell	2,133	SD 754751	98	2
Swarth Fell Pike	2,125	SD 760958	98	
Yockenthwaite Moor	2,110	SD 908810	98	30
Fell Head	2,100	SD 649982	97	
Green Hill	2,060	SD 701820	98	2
Gragareth	2,057	SD 687793	98	2
Tor Mere Top	2,050	SD 969765	98	30
Darnbrook Fell	2,047	SD 884727	98	30
Bink Moss	2,031	NY 876242	91	31
Drumaldrace	2,014	SD 873867	98	2/30
Birks Fell	c2,000*	SD 918763	98	30

The **1:50000** map column gives the Landranger Series number.
The relevant sheet numbers with their names are as follows.
91 – Appleby-in-Westmorland Area.
92 – Barnard Castle and Richmond.
97 – Kendal and Morecambe
98 – Wensleydale and Upper Wharfedale.
The **1:25000** map column gives the Outdoor Leisure sheet number.
The relevant sheet numbers with their names are as follows.
2 – Yorkshire Dales. Western Area.
10 – Yorkshire Dales. Southern Area.
30 – Yorkshire Dales. Northern and Central areas.
31 – Teesdale.
The Howgill Fells and Baugh Fell are conveniently located on Sheet SD69/79, "Sedbergh and Baugh Fell", in the Pathfinder Series.
The Mallerstang Edge Fells fall rather inconveniently on the edges of Pathfinder maps NY 80/90 and SD 89/99.
*Well, it was in the days of real Yorkshire!

TABLE 2. Ridings and Counties

Riding refers to the situation pre-April 1974.

WR – West Riding
NR – North Riding

County refers to the situation at present.

Name	Riding	County
Mickle Fell	NR	County Durham
Whernside	WR	North Yorkshire/Cumbria
Ingleborough	WR	North Yorkshire
Great Shunner Fell	NR	North Yorkshire
High Seat	NR/Westmorland	North Yorkshire/Cumbria
Great Whernside	WR	North Yorkshire
Buckden Pike	WR	North Yorkshire
Archy Styrigg	NR/Westmorland	North Yorkshire/Cumbria
Penyghent	WR	North Yorkshire
Hugh Seat	NR/Westmorland	North Yorkshire/Cumbria
Great Coum	WR	Cumbria
Long Crag	NR	County Durham
Plover Hill	WR	North Yorkshire
Baugh Fell	WR	Cumbria
The Calf	WR/Westmorland	Cumbria
Lovely Seat	NR	North Yorkshire
Calders	WR	Cumbria
Bram Rigg Top	WR	Cumbria
Great Knoutberry Hill	NR/WR	North Yorkshire/Cumbria
Rogan's Seat	NR	North Yorkshire
Fountains Fell	WR	North Yorkshire
Dodd Fell	NR	North Yorkshire
Water Crag	NR	North Yorkshire
Sails	NR	North Yorkshire
White Mossy Hill	NR	North Yorkshire/Cumbria
Simon Fell	WR	North Yorkshire
Swarth Fell Pike	WR/Westmorland	Cumbria
Yockenthwaite Moor	NR/WR	North Yorkshire
Fell Head	WR	Cumbria
Green Hill	WR/Lancashire	Cumbria
Gragareth	WR/Lancashire	North Yorkshire/Lancashire
Tor Mere Top	NR/WR	North Yorkshire
Darnbrook Fell	WR	North Yorkshire
Bink Moss	NR	County Durham
Drumaldrace	NR	North Yorkshire
Birks Fell	WR	North Yorkshire

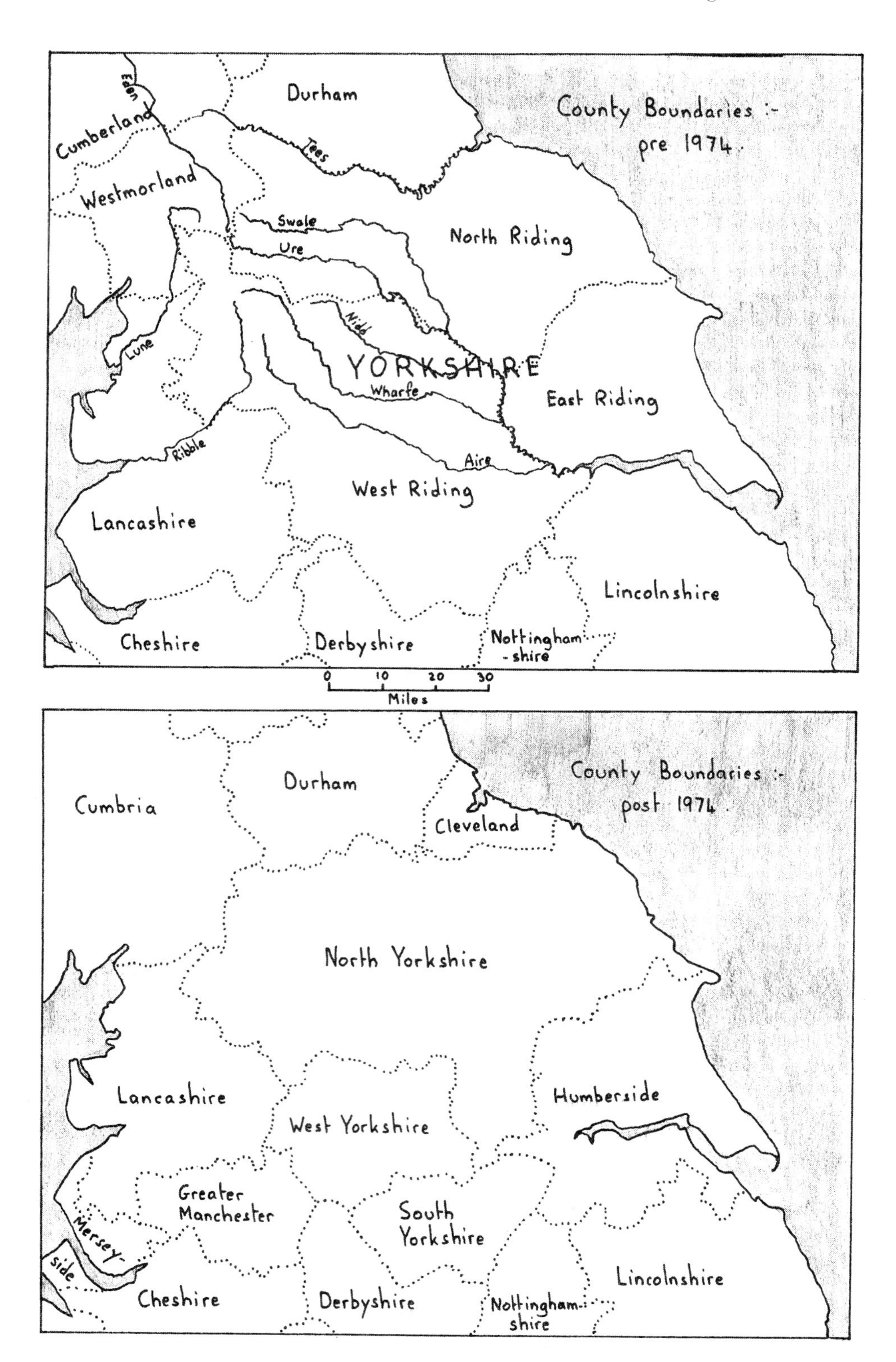
Durham
County Boundaries :-
pre 1974.
Eden
Cumberland
Tees
Westmorland
Swale
Ure
North Riding
Nidd
Lune
YORKSHIRE
Wharfe
East Riding
Ribble
Aire
West Riding
Lancashire
Lincolnshire
Cheshire
Derbyshire
Nottingham
-shire
0 10 20 30
Miles
Durham
County Boundaries :-
post 1974.
Cumbria
Cleveland
North Yorkshire
Lancashire
Humberside
West Yorkshire
Greater
Manchester
South
Yorkshire
Mersey-
side
Lincolnshire
Cheshire
Derbyshire
Nottingham-
shire

BIBLIOGRAPHY

It is impossible to write a book like this without owing a tremendous debt of gratitude to those who have walked the fells before and who have committed their experiences to paper. Pre-eminent in any list of books on Yorkshire's fells must be Harry Speight's great work *The Craven and North-West Yorkshire Highlands,*, now republished, Ella Pontefract and Marie Hartley's studies of *Wensleydale, Swaledale* and *Wharfedale,* together with Hartley's and Joan Ingilby's *The Yorkshire Dales* and the many works of Dr. Arthur Raistrick, particularly *The Pennine Dales*. Dr. Raistrick's studies of *The Lead Industry of Wensleydale and Swaledale,* his *The Face of North-West Yorkshire,* written in partnership with John Illingworth, and his many monographs on such diverse subjects as *The Story of the Pennine Walls* and *Yorkshire Maps and Map-Makers* are wonderful founts of information.

Two other authors whose works are returned to again and again are Bill Mitchell and Alfred Wainright. Mr. Mitchell has spent a working life exploring and writing about the Dales in such books as *Wild Pennines* and *The Changing Dales.* Wainright's volumes, *Walks in Limestone Country, Walks on the Howgill Fells* and *A Pennine Way Companion* are simply inimitable.

The original cause of all this wandering, and still the most inspirational book of all, is *The Mountains of England and Wales,* by George Bridge. (Gaston's Alpine Books and West Col Productions, 1973)

As well as the books mentioned above, I have found the following particularly useful:

Moorland Tramping in West Yorkshire. Alfred J. Brown (Country Life, 1931)
Odd Corners in the Yorkshire Dales. William T. Palmer (Skeffington, 1937)
The Railways of Wharfedale. Peter E. Baughan (David and Charles, 1969)
Roads and Trackways of the Yorkshire Dales. Geoffrey N. Wright, (Moorland, 1985)
Caves, Crags and Gorges. Tony Waltham (Constable, 1984)
Early Pennine Settlement. Alan King (Dalesman, 1970)
Pennine Flowers. Joan E. Duncan and R.W. Robson (Dalesman, 1977)
Pennine Birds. W.R. Mitchell and R.W. Robson (Dalesman, 1978)
English Mountain Summits. Nick Wright (Robert Hale, 1974)
The Lead Smelting Mills of the Yorkshire Dales. Robert T. Clough (Author, 1962)
The Yorkshire Dales – A Walkers Guide to the National Park. Gladys Sellers (Cicerone Press)
Settle-Carlisle Railway. W.R. Mitchell and David Joy (Dalesman, 1966)
The Story of the Settle-Carlisle Line. Frederick W. Houghton and W. Hubert Foster (Norman Arch, 1948)
The Midland Railway – Its Rise and Progress. Frederick S. Williams (Bemrose, 1877)

In preparing this book I have explored the reference libraries in Skipton and Leeds as well as the fell tops above the Skirfare and Lune. They always seem to put the reference departments in libraries upstairs so all my research has led me in the right direction!

Pinnacle Rock, Penyghent. (Bill Pates)